DETOX THE MIND

RAJINDER SINGH

RADIANCE PUBLISHERS

Radiance Publishers

1042 Maple Ave.

Lisle, Illinois 60532

Website: www.radiancepublishers.com

Email: sales@radiancepublishers.com

3   5   7   9   11   12   10   8   6   4   2

© Copyright 2022 by Radiance Publishers

ISBN 978-0-918224-31-6

Library of Congress Control Number: 2020916169

Printed in Canada by Premier.ca

DETOX
THE MIND

RAJINDER SINGH

Other Books by Rajinder Singh

Meditation as Medication for the Soul

Inner and Outer Peace through Meditation

(with Foreword by H.H. the Dalai Lama)

Empowering Your Soul through Meditation

Building Bridges through Meditation

Echoes of the Divine

In Hindi

Spirituality in Modern Times

True Happiness

Self Realization

Search for Peace within the Soul

Spiritual Treasures

Spiritual Talks

Praise for Sant Rajinder Singh's Books

"Sant Rajinder Singh Ji explains how peace can be created through meditation and inner reflection. There will be no lasting peace unless individual human beings have some sense of inner peace. To create inner peace it is necessary to calm the mind, hence the importance of meditation. I greatly appreciate Sant Rajinder Singh Ji's contribution here to the goal of peace that we are all working towards. May readers of this book find peace within themselves through meditation and so foster a greater sense of peace throughout the world."
— H.H. the Dalai Lama

"This outstanding handbook reflects Rajinder Singh's deep wisdom and realization emerging from divine love and inner fulfillment."
— Deepak Chopra

"This book by Sant Rajinder Singh, replete with many delightful examples, brilliantly lights up a pathway bridging the materialistic world of science and our inner selves."
— T. Colin Campbell, Ph.D., Professor Emeritus, Cornell University, and author of *Whole* and *The China Study* (co-authored with T M Campbell)

"A powerful, deep, clearly written book about practical spirituality that helps us let go of the self-made blocks that interfere with the awareness that we are one with God and each other, that there is no separation, and that our soul is present and fully alive forever."
— Gerald G. Jampolsky, M.D., author: *Love Is Letting Go of Fear*

"Firmly rooted in traditional wisdom, the author faces contemporary questions and challenges squarely and in a non-sectarian way... to bring the seed of peace within us to fruition in daily life and the world we live in."
— Brother David-Steindl Rast

"Rajinder Singh's new book is food for the soul. It is an inspiring and informative source that speaks to both beginners and experienced travelers on the path of life. I was uplifted as I read this book and re-dedicate myself to honoring my inner work."
   – Steven Halpern, Educator, Recording Artist, and Musician

"Meditation empowers us in two spiritual arenas. First, it leads us to inner peace and fulfillment.... Second, meditation allows us to use our talents and skills to make the world a better place to live. Rajinder Singh elaborates on these ideas beautifully. He says that by mastering meditation, we not only attain personal fulfillment, but we also become an instrument for bringing peace and joy to those around us."
   – Mary Nurrie Stearns, Editor, Personal Transformation

"Rajinder Singh expounds his theory that true peace and happiness can only come from within: The skill lies in learning how to tap into them."
   – Here's Health magazine

"Sant Rajinder Singh's newest contribution, *Detox the Mind*, provides an individual-based strategy to improve humanity. This book empowers honest self-discovery! The challenge he sets forth and the tools provided at the individual level will improve the collective good, one person at a time."
   – Terry Mason, M.D., retd. COO,
   Cook County Department of Public Health

Table of Contents

PART 1:

What Is Detoxing the Mind?

A Tranquil Life of Relaxation and Joy Can Be Ours

A life free from stress, fear, anxiety, and depression awaits us. We can awake looking forward to a day filled with peace and joy. Imagine how wonderful life could be if we could replace stress with relaxation and happiness. We can take simple steps to make this dream a reality.

Picture the tranquility of a crystal-clear lake reflecting breathtaking scenery. Immersing into its still waters, calmness washes over us. Stress melts, replaced with profound well-being. Love and joy bubble up within. All our problems fade away as we float into the sea of love, happiness, and bliss.

There is a tranquil lake of profound relaxation within us. Unfortunately, many cannot experience it, as it is covered with toxins and pollution, making it inaccessible.

By following a step-by-step plan, we can dive into an inner sea of relaxation anytime we want and lead a joyous, peaceful life. The journey begins with removing obstacles to finding our inner spa. Those who want to improve their physical health and well-being go through a process called detoxification or ridding themselves of impurities. Yet, even after a physical detoxification, we may still suffer from mental stress, anxiety, fear, depression, hopelessness, and unhappiness. There is no need to turn to drugs and alcohol and suffer their adverse side effects to be happy. We can rid ourselves of the mental blockages that keep us from experiencing peace and happiness. By detoxing our mind, we can experience a life of lasting joy and peace.

Freeing ourselves of mental stress and fears opens us to an even greater reward. It clears our mind to experience the spiritual treasures of our soul. A toxic mind blocks our connection to the wellspring of unconditional love, ecstasy, and peace. Detoxing our mind enables us to dive into a pool of all-embracing love, bliss, and joy within.

People worldwide are turning to meditation as a way to detox the mind to achieve peace and happiness. This practical how-to book guides us through simple methods of meditation to replace our stress with blissful relaxation. Throughout the chapters are action plans and exercises that can help us focus on steps we can take to detox our mind and bathe in the nourishing peace and joy within.

– Rajinder Singh

CHAPTER 1:

What is Detoxification?

In our quest for peace and happiness, we often meet obstacles. Some of the challenges that prevent us from leading a life of tranquility relate to our physical body. Living with pain and discomfort in our body makes it difficult to feel at peace. This drives us to seek solutions to restore our physical health. As toxins build up in the body they cause dysfunction in our organs. This can result in pain and feeling unwell. One means of being proactive to restore our physical health is detoxing our body.

Detoxifying our body is only one part of the equation for us to attain peace and joy. Our mind poses challenges to our happiness. Throughout the day, we are bombarded by thoughts that affect us mentally and emotionally. While we may have succeeded in detoxing our body, we may still feel agitated and under stress in our mind. Can we apply the same solution of detoxing our body to detoxifying our mind? Will detoxing our mind lead to the mental peace and happiness we seek? This book seeks to provide tools to apply in our lives so we can take steps to attain happiness and tranquility.

First, let's look at the differences between detoxifying our body and our mind.

Detoxification of the Body

Some physical ailments can be traced to toxic substances within our human body. The main cleansing organs in our body are the liver and kidneys. Their main function is to rid the body of built-up toxins that impact our health. By eliminating or reducing the toxic load in our body, we can free ourselves of various illnesses.

Often times, people choose to ingest toxic substances, such as alcohol, tobacco, and hallucinogenic drugs, which are known to be hazardous to our health. Many of the foods and beverages we consume are filled with toxins of which most of us are unaware. As toxins build up in our system, it leads to organ dysfunction and even failure. Environmental toxins are a by-product of living in an industrialized world. We are all exposed to varying levels of environmental pollutants based upon the part of the world in which we live.

We can achieve detoxification by various means:

- **Medical detoxification** involves using nutrition, diet, medication or technology to rid the body of toxins. The detoxification of heavy metals occurs primarily in the liver. Detoxification is also used to remove chemical substances that are addictive, such as drugs and alcohol, from the body. When the toxic load in the kidneys increases, the kidneys cannot eliminate excess water, solutes, and toxins from the blood naturally. When the kidneys completely fail, then a dialysis machine is used to artificially act as a kidney and remove toxins from the system.

• Preventative medicine avoids or eliminates toxins before they create health problems.

• Alternative methods detox the body using more natural methods. Among these are herbal or vitamin supplements, electromagnetic treatments, body-cleansing, fasting, chelation therapy (heavy metal detoxification), and metabolic therapy, amongst others. These treatments accelerate the detoxifying capability of the body and thus may also lead to the loss of essential elements. Supervision by a medical professional is recommended.

The results of physical detoxification are improved bodily health and wellness. It is a stepping-stone to disease prevention.

Detoxification of the Mind

While medical advances have uncovered causes of many physical diseases and offer treatments, what are the causes of and solutions for the toxins that affect our mind?

What is the mechanism by which toxins affect our mind?

In this connection, there is a story about a teacher known for helping students achieve concentration. They had been working for months to learn and still had not achieved mastery. One of their friends inquired as to why they were taking so long to learn one skill.

A student said, "It is not that easy."

The friend said, "Maybe you are not as smart as me. With my intelligence, it won't take me long to learn it. Take me to your teacher." The student brought him to class and asked the teacher to help his friend learn concentration.

The teacher told the student to go into the forest to practice mental focus.

The teacher said, "For your assignment, take drawing paper and a pencil, and find a pond of still water in the woods. Look at your reflection in that pond and draw your own face."

The student agreed that it seemed easy enough to do. Then the teacher added one more requirement.

"Also bring with you a sack of pebbles. As you look at your reflection in the still water, you must throw a pebble into the water each time any thought enters your mind. The thoughts can be of any kind, but as soon as each one arises, toss in the small stone. When you are able to see your reflection clearly in the pond, draw what you see, and bring the picture back to me."

The student felt encouraged that the second task would be easy, and he would have no trouble drawing his image reflected back in the water.

Finding a small pond, the new student sat down and set out the paper and pencil. With the sack of pebbles by his side, he leaned over the edge to see his image. No sooner had he done that, when he remembered what he had done with his friends the previous day.

"Oh, oh," he said, "There's a thought." Reaching into his sack, he picked up a pebble and threw it into the water. Swirling ripples radiated from the pebble, and he could not see his own reflection.

When the water became still, he again looked in to see his face, but this time he started making plans of what he wanted to do in the evening. Realizing he was thinking again, he threw another pebble into the water. Again, the ripples marred the tranquility of the pool and his face was not clear.

"This may be harder than I thought," he said. When the ripples subsided, he tried again, but this time, recalling a disagreement he had with a fellow student, he mentally began criticizing him. Recognizing that his thoughts were agitated, he threw in another pebble. Each time he had to wait until the ripples stopped, so he could try to see his face again.

This continued for hours. Sometimes when he recalled good fortune, other thoughts of jealousy arose. Other times he worried about the health of his parents. Many types of thoughts crept into his mind, each forcing him to throw in a stone that disturbed the calm waters.

The student grew frustrated that he could not peer into the water even once without a thought causing him to throw a pebble into the pond. After a full day, he returned to his teacher without a drawing.

When the teacher asked to see the picture of his face, the student said, "I did not find a single moment without any thoughts. The day passed with a continual stream of them caus-ing me to toss in a pebble and upset the tranquility of the water."

The teacher smiled and said, "Now you can see why your friends are taking so long to master this skill. Thoughts are like waves in the ocean that continually flow to the shore, making it difficult for the ocean to ever be calm enough to see our clear reflection in it."

This story illustrates the difficulties in staying free of stress and worries. The continual flow of thoughts occupies our attention. Toxic thoughts are like pebbles thrown into water, causing ripples that disturb our peace of mind.

What are the various toxins that affect our mind and cause us stress and pain? What causes these toxins to disturb our mental state? What are safe and natural methods to rid ourselves of these toxins to gain relief from life's mental and emotional pains?

Toxins that Cause Mental Pain and Suffering

When have we felt completely at peace? When did we experience a time when no one or nothing disturbed us? Have we ever felt tranquility through every pore of our being? When has contentment filled us? In what states have we enjoyed happiness and calm? If we have ever had these experiences, did they result in:

- renewed energy and a zest for life?
- feeling connected to others and to nature?
- our heart and soul expanding to feel oneness to others and the universe?
- love blossoming from our inner self?

We would all love to be in that state. It is our natural condition of well-being. Our inner nature is one of peace, happiness, contentment, and freedom from stress. We can live each moment of our lives in this state of joy. It is possible to hold onto these moments and make them a part of each second of our life.

Mental equilibrium is possible. People can achieve such states of happiness. We need to detox our mind to achieve such a state.

Becoming aware of our mental toxins is the first step. Here is a list of common toxins that affect our mind.

- anger
- hatred
- criticism
- violent thoughts
- intolerance
- prejudice and bigotry
- egotism

- jealousy and envy
- greed and possessiveness
- selfishness
- lying
- deceit
- hypocrisy
- desires

- attachment
- obsession
- fear
- anxiety
- panic
- stress and worry about the past
- worry about the future

There may be others we can add from our own experiences. Any of these can become toxic in our mind.

Becoming Conscious of Our Mental Toxins

Many people are aware that they are not feeling peaceful and happy but may be unconscious of the reason. It is easier to be aware of what makes us physically uncomfortable. For example, we are aware of the itch when a mosquito bites. We know how our stomach feels when we eat something rancid. We sneeze when we catch a cold. But how many of us are aware of the effect on our mind when various mental toxins affect us? By becoming conscious of these toxins, we can take steps to avoid their effects to preserve our mental well-being.

Exercise: Review the list of toxins in this chapter. Make a list of the ones that have affected your peace of mind. Make a second list called "Goals to Detox My Mind" and write down the ones you would like to be free of as you work through this book.

CHAPTER 2:

Types of Toxins that Affect Our Mind

Do we work at a job where there is so much to do that sometimes we don't know if we are coming or going? We may be in the middle of completing one task when more deadlines for other tasks land on our desk. Feeling we cannot meet the deadlines, we then work overtime. There is so much work that we must take it home. In addition, the constant pings of emails or text message alerts interrupt us and consume our time.

Maybe we run a household. Our schedule of taking care of a family looks like an air traffic control chart. We run from one chore to the next, driving our family from one activity to another and can barely catch our breath.

On top of work and home, there's a continual flow of tasks just to survive. We must take care of our health, finances, relationships, community responsibilities, and other duties. There is too much to do in so little time. The result is living in a constant state of pressure and stress. There is barely time to take a break or a vacation. This continual multitasking and rushing to meet deadlines reaches a point where our mind is so filled with stress that our health and well-being are affected.

Relationships with others—whether at work, at home, with our friends, with loved ones, with neighbors, or interacting with others in all spheres of life—can pose challenges. Everyone has his or her own background and ways of thinking and behaving. Not everyone thinks, speaks, and acts as we do. Whenever we interact with others who have a different point of view, those who have not learned the art of adjustment, collaboration, and compromise often experience stress. We may feel mental anguish when we have to give in to another's way of thinking or doing something, or we end up trying to get our way. All these add to the mental stress of life.

While there are many types of toxins, they all have a similar effect. Mental toxins color our world view and how we experience life.

There is a story about a father and his grown son who wanted to spend quality time together. As his father had worked hard all his life with little time to travel, the son bought tickets for a trip to faraway lands.

Their first stop was a mountainous region with spectacular scenery. The son thought the breathtaking views from the mountaintops with refreshing streams flowing through pine forests would excite his father. As the son joyfully took panoramic photos, the father lacked enthusiasm.

"What's wrong?" asked the son.

The father said, "I don't know why you brought me here. The sky is dark and cloudy. The streams look polluted and filthy. I know you mean well, but this is a dreary place."

Hoping the next vacation spot would be better, the son flew his father to a sunny beach along the ocean. Delighted with the blue-green ocean and the pristine sands, the son took photos to keep as happy memories. However, again the father seemed disappointed.

"What kind of place is this?" asked the father. "The ocean has debris and pollution. The sand is so dirty, I don't want to sit here."

Confused at his father's disappointment, the son thought maybe the next vacation spot would be more to his liking. They visited a forest with lovely botanical gardens.

Strolling through the gardens there was an array of flowers of all colors, shapes, and sizes. Again, the son was engaged with taking memorable photos.

The father remarked, "You spend all this money to come to this garden. But I think the flowers in my house are more colorful and beautiful than these. How can they charge so much money for the entry fees to see such dull and lifeless plants?"

After the trip, they returned to the home of the father.

The son said, "I am sorry the trip was so disappointing to you. I don't understand. We saw so many beautiful sights and you complained about each of them."

The son printed out all the photos he took to remind his father of everything they saw.

The father said, "What did you do to these photos? Did you enhance the photos with software to make each place look better than it was?"

The son said, "Absolutely not. This is exactly as each place looked."

The father replied, "Your photos show bright, clean, and beautiful places. That is not what I saw on the trip. You must have altered the images before you printed the photos."

It was then that the son realized something: When they were looking at the photos, his father removed his glasses.

"Dad, you are near-sighted. You were wearing your distance glasses for the whole trip." The son inspected his father's glasses, holding them up to the light.

"Look at this!" exclaimed the son, "These lenses are not only filthy, but they have cracks in them. No wonder you didn't enjoy any of the sights. You were seeing everything through dirty and damaged lenses."

The experience of the father describes how we experience the world. Our daily life is colored by the lens of our mental outlook. If the lens of our thoughts is clean, we see things as they are. But if our lens is filled with toxins, then we experience those poisons in our life. As a result, we may suffer from unhappiness, stress, anxiety, and fear. When these reach an unbearable level, it can cause us to experience depression, hopelessness, helplessness, and panic attacks.

By understanding the types of toxins that affect our mind, we can eliminate them and reduce the stresses of life. We can learn to relax and stay calm for improved health and wellness.

By detoxing our mind, we can learn to handle stress and dip into the pool of relaxation within.

Exercise: List the sources of stress in your life. Add any not described in this chapter. Then, list personal benefits you would like to achieve by eliminating those stresses. Think about the various toxins that plague your mind. Then, identify the effect each plays in your life as a first step to overcoming them. While this chapter is meant to raise awareness of which toxins affect you mentally, Part 3 of this book will provide solutions to apply to your life to detox your mind.

PART 2:

Benefits of Detoxing Your Mind:

Keys to Health, Success, Happiness, and Peace

CHAPTER 3:

Boost Your Physical Health

Medical research reveals a correlation between our body and mind. Our mental state affects our physical health. Our physical health affects our mind. Thus, mental toxins have an adverse effect on the health and wellness of our body. If we want to reduce our risk of contracting varied diseases, we can take action to reduce our mental toxins.

Anatomy of a Stress-Related Illness Caused by Mental Toxins

If we scan the list of toxins, we find they all lead to similar outcomes. We enter a state of stress. Whether it is anger, ego, greed, attachment, worry about the past or future, or any other state of unease, our mind triggers the stress response.

Our heart rate increases with readiness to run or fight. Blood vessels contract to pump blood harder to reach our legs to run and to our arms to defend ourselves. Breathing constricts. Our stomach goes into knots. The adrenal glands pump adrenaline and cortisol into our system. What was meant to be a survival response to a threat to our life can also trigger a natural reaction to any mental toxin we face.

If we undergo this stress response once in a while, our body can handle it because we return to our normal, stress-free, relaxed state when the threat ends. However, when we live in a continual state of fear and anxiety every day, it can have a harmful effect on our body.

Medical researchers have studied the effect of stress on our physical health. They have traced certain diseases to stress. Among these are heart disease, cardiovascular disease, stroke, stomach disorders, headaches, skin conditions, hormonal problems, and many others. The excessive flow of cortisol and adrenaline through our system causes a breakdown of various bodily systems. Because of its side effects, doctors only prescribe medicinal cortisone for short-term use as a last resort for certain conditions. Yet, mental toxins put us at risk for cortisol's dangerous side effects when stress causes it to flow as a continual stream through our body, day after day. This produces a domino effect. Our physical reaction to mental stressors causes us to develop stress-related illnesses that require medicines with their own side effects. Then, those medicines have their own side effects which might result in us needing still other medications to counter the initial medication. A downward spiral begins, which could have been avoided or reduced if we had controlled the initial problem—our mental toxins.

As children, we learn that if we put our hand on the stove we will be burned. All it may take is one experience to teach us not to repeat that. If we realize that giving in to mental toxins could lead us down the road to physical illnesses, we may choose to break the habit of engaging in thoughts that lead to mental stress.

Physical Benefits of Detoxing Our Mind

By controlling our mental toxins, we can reduce our risk of stress-related physical illnesses. This increases our chances of enjoying improved health and wellness. Our heart rate and breathing will work at a stress-free pace. Fight or flight hormones will not surge through us, thereby reducing damage to our organs. Without stress, our bodily systems run more smoothly. We can easily wind down from periodic stress to return to our natural state of calm and tranquility. A feel-good cycle begins. When we feel physically well, our mind is more peaceful. When our mind is at peace, our stress decreases, contributing to improved physical health.

When we practice controlling the flow of mental toxins, we feel better physically and mentally. This incentive of feeling good motivates us to want to repeat being in a happy frame of mind so we can take control over toxins that affect us physically. Over time, we become stronger and better able to resist falling victim to those toxins.

Detoxing our mind can prevent and reduce the effects of stress-related ailments to improve our physical health.

Exercise: Reflect on times that your stress resulted in physical illnesses. Measure your pulse, heart rate, or breathing rate when stressed out and compare them to times when you feel calm and peaceful. You may want to start a log in which you track your daily stress and note if it affects your physical health in some way.

CHAPTER 4:

Enjoy Mental and Emotional Health

Polluting our mind with toxins can lead to problems that affect our mental and emotional health. We enter a vicious cycle caused by our thoughts causing stress-related illnesses. The pain and suffering from the illness can trigger more mental and emotional problems. Hormonal imbalance caused by stress can lead to ailments that affect our mental and emotional state. A host of psychological problems are related to brain chemistry. Many are physiological and require prescription medications. While some mental and emotional problems may be due to genetics, others may find their roots in environmental causes or body chemistry resulting from stress. If we could reduce our stress, we may be able to reduce stress-related illnesses that affect our mental and emotional states.

Toxins such as hatred, criticism, and violent thoughts can escalate into rage and fury. If we live in such an angry frame of mind, it can lead to emotional problems. For example, anger and rage affect our relationships with family, friends, neighbors, co-workers, and even strangers. When we light the match of anger, it can quickly escalate into a raging, out-of-control fire. When others react to our anger with their own negativity and rage, we become hurt and upset. Thinking that we have done nothing wrong, we cannot understand their reaction to us and why the relationship has taken a downward turn. We could have found a calm and peaceful way to work out a problem rather than letting it burst into flames, leaving us emotionally scarred.

Consider the effects that intolerance, prejudice, and bigotry have on our emotional and mental states. We become filled with disdain towards people who are different from us. Whether it is how others look, act, or the language they speak, prejudice may lead us to act negatively towards those who are not like us. This creates barriers between people and ruins relationships. Our mind then pigeonholes people into stereotypes. We enter a cycle where we either avoid people or lash out at them for being different. When we interact daily with many people who are different from us, it is hard to get through a day peacefully, when the toxins of prejudice, intolerance, and bigotry pollute our mind.

Think of the effects that untruthfulness, lying, deceit, and hypocrisy have on our mental and emotional state. When we try to hide the truth whether in word or action, or we pretend to be something we are not, we are filled with the toxins of fear, anxiety, and even panic. Why? We are always worried about someone finding out the truth we are trying to suppress. When keeping a lie going consistently, we live in the grip of fear of being caught. If someone were to find us out, there may be consequences. Our integrity and reputation may be destroyed. No one will trust or believe us in the future. Even if we tell the truth in other situations, people will be suspicious if even once they found we had not been honest. Thus, we enter a tailspin of anxiety, fear, and panic that keeps us mentally and emotionally upset.

When we worry about the past or future, we may become so obsessed with those thoughts that we lose the ability to function normally. We cannot focus on our work, our loved ones, or our health. Some people enter into depression and cannot function normally in day-to-day life. Becoming so consumed with regretting a past we cannot change, or inventing scenarios that may or may not happen in the future, we become emotionally upset. It is hard to be peaceful when consumed with toxins caused by worry.

If we take any other toxin—such as greed, ego, envy, jealousy, attachment, possessiveness, selfishness, or desires—we can trace its effects to emotional and mental pains.

If flooded with greed, our mind is in a state of conniving how to get more or to take from others. This can affect our loving relationships with others if we see them as sources of supply for our greediness rather than as human beings to love and cherish. When filled with ego, our thoughts, words, and deeds are consumed by trying to boost ourselves higher than others. This can mar our emotional relationships with others when they are hurt when we treat them as our inferiors. These conflicts between people ruin loving relationships, affecting our mental and emotional state.

Attachment to our possessions at the expense of our relationships can result in interactions that cause us mental or emotional pain and problems. If we are possessive of others and treat people as if we own them, that can result in reactions that create barriers and distance between hearts.

Mental and Emotional Benefits of Detoxing Our Mind

Imagine awakening each day to the sun shining through a blue sky dotted with fluffy white clouds. A crystal-clear lake peacefully reflects the colors of the sky. Fragrant gardens of blossoming flowers delight the eye. Gentle fountains bubble into streams that flow through the garden. Music that delights our heart plays. Joy fills us. Our mind is calm. Our spirit is filled with happiness and love. This is our natural state of mental and emotional stability.

We can live in this peaceful state by detoxing our mind. It does not mean that life won't throw us challenges. No one can escape those. But when we learn to detox our mind, we can deal with them in a way that does not put our mind and emotions into turmoil. We may be aware that we have a problem, but we don't let it affect our emotional and mental balance.

When we learn to detox our mind from these poisons, we find a reduction in mental or emotional pains. We will then be on the road to mental and emotional stability and a life of happiness.

Exercise: Which of the mental and emotional stresses in this chapter occupy your attention? Reflect on the ones that cause you the most distress. If there are more than one, list in priority order with a commitment to taking steps as you work through this book to eliminate them.

CHAPTER 5:

Achieve Academic, Career, Job, and Sports Success

Along with physical, mental, and emotional benefits, detoxing our mind can dramatically improve our outer life. It can help us achieve academic, career, job, or sports success.

The underlying principal for detoxing the mind is reducing stress. Studies point to the effects stress has on the brain. First, it shifts our attention from the higher cognitive and logical portion of the brain—the prefrontal lobes—that helps us perform executive functions such as planning, solving problems, and making rational decisions. This is the part of the brain in which we function most optimally when learning and studying, working at our job, playing sports, or engaging in any creative endeavor.

When we undergo stress from the toxins that pollute our

mind, we enter states of fear, anxiety, or panic. This shifts our attention from the higher cognitive part of the brain to the reptilian part of the brain that is more reactive. The reptilian part of the brain is the one that sets in motion the fight or flight response. When we are in fear and preparing our body to fight or run, we are not in the logical, rational part of the brain required for studies, work, or achievement in our hobbies. Instead, we are in a mode in which we feel threatened and are focused on survival.

To perform well at school, work, sports, or hobbies, we want to function from the part of the brain that requires concentration, focus, planning, and logic. These help us perform well in our studies, job, or a sport. Detoxing the mind helps us stay in the zone of optimal performance. It keeps us from dipping into the part of the brain where we are only reacting in fear to whatever threat we perceive faces us. Is our life really threatened by our children leaving their toys all over our home office? If a co-worker leaves a used coffee cup in the office sink, is it the end of the world? If we allow these small inconveniences in life to make our brain toxic with anger, triggering reactions that draw us into the reptilian brain, it prevents us from doing our work well. If we could detox our mind, we could always remain calm and thus perform better at school, our job, or our sports or hobbies.

While many brain studies show the effect that a calm mind has on performance academically, at work, or during sports, we will only believe it if we try the experiment ourselves. Can we recall a time when we tried to read or study, but our mind was in a state of fear about some situation? Did this result in our struggling to complete the assignment or test? Reflect on times at work when our job descriptions required our full attention to perform those tasks. When beset by toxic thoughts, did work come easy? Or were we distracted and lost concentration on our work or studies? Did we have to give up doing the task due to stress and miss our deadline? These are a few examples to show the importance of detoxing the mind.

People engaged in sports notice what happens when lost in stressful thoughts. For example, golfers who are thinking about something else or are upset over their last poor shot may find that during the moment they are supposed to strike the golf ball they lose focus and do not perform well on this current shot. Part of the success of a golf shot requires total concentration without distraction of other thoughts. The mechanics of the golf swing requires full focus. Being lost in the mind's toxins can interfere with that. The same is true whether hitting a baseball, shooting a basketball into a hoop, kicking a soccer ball, throwing a football, playing cricket, or performing well in any other sport or game.

Benefits of Detoxing the Mind for Success in Academics, Job or Career, or Sports

Consider the difference it makes in one's academic life when one gets a high score on a test or good grade in a course. Scoring low often means retaking a test, redoing an assignment, restudying, or repeating a course. High grades are often rewarded. It can mean admission into a special honors or advanced program, acceptance to a college or university, or even a scholarship that pays for the tuition for our education. It is hard enough to study for a test or course. We can increase our performance when not bathed in toxins that cause mental stress and decrease our focus. When calm during our academic work or tests, we perform better. Remaining in the cognitive part of the brain, we can access the information we studied more quickly and efficiently. It keeps us from relapsing into negativity that sends us into the reptilian part of the brain where we cannot concentrate on our course. The benefits of detoxing our brain are many for those who want to achieve academic success.

In this age of technology, the landscape of our jobs and careers is always shifting. Each new advancement requires acquiring new skills on the job. Whereas in the past, we may have had one job for our entire life, modern technology may cause us to have a number of career changes in our lifetime. Jobs we used to do become updated or phased out. Jobs that never existed before offer new opportunities. Learning on the job is a new part of life. This requires us to extend our education into our career or work. We may graduate school with a set of skills, but when hired we have to go through more training and onboarding to add more skills. Anyone involved with technology knows that the computer software we finally mastered gets updated regularly and we have to learn changes made to the program. Jobs that used to be manual now may be done by computer which needs to be learned. With automation, jobs previously done physically are now performed by robots or machines using software programs we have to master. The stakes are high because our income depends on us knowing and performing our job well. Competition is fierce, and we must keep up with the demands and expectations put on us, including meeting quotas and deadlines. Detoxing our mind can mean the difference between keeping our job, getting promoted, or even losing our job due to poor performance. If we can detox our mind, we can concentrate better on our work. We can be more efficient and productive. This ensures that we can perform well on our job or in our careers and reap the many benefits such as financial success, job growth, promotions, and job satisfaction. Being able to concentrate and do well at work opens new doors to us as we seek the job and careers we want.

Sports and hobbies play a large part of modern life. While schools offered recess, physical education, plus art and music classes in the past, over time these evolved into clubs and sports teams. No longer engaging in these just for fun, the stakes of sports teams or competition in the arts and music have become fierce. Winning is often tied to one's self-esteem and how others look at us. Increased competition in professional sports, arts, and music has crept into colleges, high school, middle, and elementary schools. Intense practice schedules and competitions require participants to excel for themselves and their team. Thus, attention must be paid to performing well in one's chosen pastime. Detoxing our mind helps us focus better on our sports or hobbies such as music, art, or any other endeavor. For some, doing well is a source of personal pride in doing our best. For others, it means being a good team player to bring about a win. Others are trying to gain a scholarship into a university. Some rely on sports, art, or music for income. For whatever reason we participate in a sport or hobby, keeping our mind free of toxins while engaging in it can contribute to achieving success.

Whether attending school or college, working at our job or in our career, or engaging in a hobby or sport, detoxing our mind offers long-term benefits leading to the joys of a successful and happy life.

Exercise: Remember a time in which you tried to study when your mind was in a state of fear about some situation. Or recall a time when your work required your full attention. Could you focus on it when your mind was engaged in toxic thoughts? Or did you find yourself distracted? Did you lose concentration on what you were doing, make mistakes, or not complete the job by the deadline? Recall a time when engaged in a sport or hobby in which distractions from toxic thoughts interfered with your success. Jot down how much better you could have performed in academics, at work, or in a sport or hobby when your mind was not filled with mental toxins.

CHAPTER 6:

Improve Your Relationships

No matter how close our relationships with family, friends, loved ones, co-workers, or neighbors are, bumps in the road always arise. No two people think alike. Eventually, there are bound to be disagreements and arguments in even the closest relationships. Sometimes we can weather them and return to being congenial and close; but other times we cannot deal with them and the relationship cools or even splits apart.

The pain we experience from what should be a joyful closeness can be unbearable. Anguish, confusion, despair, and disillusionment swirl in our heads. Relationship problems are so debilitating that people can sink into deep emotional pain or depression. It can affect one's ability to concentrate on our studies or work, and even in taking care of our physical needs. Our appetite, interest in life, and physical well-being can be affected.

Parents can suffer problems with their children, and vice versa. We may go through ups and downs in our relationships with partners, spouses, or significant others. We can have trouble with immediate family members and relatives. Friends can undergo difficulties with each other. Sometimes, neighbors don't see eye to eye. At work, we may struggle with our bosses, co-workers, or employees.

No matter what difficulties we encounter with others, it replays in our mind and affects our feelings. Some problems are easily resolved while others can be prolonged. It clouds our peace of mind and heart. Is there any way to prevent or resolve the pain caused by toxins that affect our relationships?

Benefits of Detoxing Our Mind to Improve Relationships

When we have a pain in the body, whether a headache or stomachache, we can take a pain reliever. Is there anything we can take for a pain in our heart from relationship problems?

Problems with others often result from the relationship being poisoned by mental toxins. There are multiple causes for these toxins to attack. Our closeness with someone can be affected by anger, greed, jealousy, ego, or selfishness. There is no one cause for these problems. There are many ways that a relationship can suffer. Sometimes multiple toxins complicate the issue. The key is to detox our mind from these poisons to keep our relationships smooth and positive. There is a way to lessen and eliminate problems we have with others that can affect our peace and happiness.

Detoxing our mind ensures smooth sailing along our journey with others on the sea of life. Issues arise in every relationship. No two people see things the same way. Everyone has a different perspective. When we detox our minds, we can accept that other people look at things differently, which will eliminate much of the tension between two people.

In any household there are bound to be differences of opinion on how much money to spend for everyday needs. Common questions in a family surround the amount of money spent on clothing, food, home furnishings, the children's education, or vacations. After bills are paid, how do we spend what is left over? Do we save or spend on other things we want? In dealing with these, they can be discussed in a calm manner, or they can escalate into arguments. Often arguments result in unkind words being said that hurt the other person. That results in retaliatory words that bring pain. Then, instead of arguing about the initial problem, we are hurling abusive words on each other or extending the fighting into other unrelated areas. By the time the parties are done, they do not even remember what they were initially arguing about.

Similar situations go on in an office or place of work. Co-workers or bosses and workers may not agree on the best way to handle a job. They can discuss the pros and cons of each course of action in a calm way. But unfortunately, that too can escalate into heated words. Instead of looking at all the angles, the discussion can turn into angry words. One co-worker then finds fault and criticizes the other. Or, to retaliate, one runs to the boss to complain about the other person making their life difficult. They may seek to undermine each other, which can even result in someone else losing their job.

Whenever people are together in any kind of relationship, whether work or social, there are bound to be different points of view. In trying to decide on where to go on a night out, some may want to go to a movie, while others to a restaurant or a sports event. There can be a friendly discussion to decide, but when we don't get our way we might dig in and turn it into an angry fight.

All these situations then weigh on our mind. The repercussions of a fight continue for a long time after the last words are spoken. They linger not only in our minds, but it can affect our emotions and our psychological balance. The more we dwell on it, the more we want to seek revenge against those who spoke angry words to us. This goes on for days, weeks, months, and sometimes years.

How can we prevent relationship problems from affecting our peace of mind and spiritual progress?

There is a story about a father and mother who had taken their children sightseeing. As they walked through a zoo, each had different interests and wished to go their separate ways. They agreed to meet at a certain time at a central place at which stood a large statue of a great hero from the past.

The parents reached there first, with the father coming from one direction and the mother arriving from another side. They stopped on opposite sides of the statue to admire it.

The father said, "Do you see the shield of this knight glistening in the sun? It must be made of pure gold."

The mother then reacted and said, "What is wrong with you? That shield is not gold; it is silver."

The father said, "How can you disagree with me? Something is wrong with you!"

The mother said, "I am the smart one in the family. You must be stupid thinking it is gold. You should get your eyes checked!"

The father then bounced back with cruel words for the wife. Then, the wife retaliated with angry words toward her husband. Soon, they were in a heated argument going back and forth about how terrible each other was.

As they argued, their children showed up at the statue.

The son asked, "What are you two fighting about?"

The daughter said, "Yes, from far away in the zoo, we could hear you fighting. You are disturbing the peace of this place. What is the problem?"

The father said, "Your mother doesn't know what she is talking about. She thinks the shield is made of silver."

The mother said, "Your father is so stubborn and won't admit I am right. The shield is clearly made of silver."

The two again began fighting, with one declaring it silver and the other gold.

Finally, the children became fed up and looked carefully at the statue's shield.

The daughter said to her mother, "Come around and stand on the side of the statue where Dad is."

The son said to his father, "And you come around and stand on the side of the statue where Mom is standing."

Both father and mother exchanged sides.

Suddenly, they both hung their heads in shame. The side of

the shield on the mother's side was silver; and the side of the shield on the father's side was gold.

The son said, "See, Mom and Dad, you were both right."

The daughter added, "Each of you were standing on the opposite side of the statue, so from your side you were correct in what you were looking at. You were both right from your point of view. But you were both wrong to fight about it."

The wisdom of the children in this story is a good example of how easily a relationship is destroyed by the toxins that plague our mind. Amongst them is a failure to see another's point of view. We see things one way, but others have a different point of view. We then try to convince the other that we are right and he or she is wrong.

If we can detox our mind to deal with disagreements, the outcome would be far different. Rather than digging in that we are right and that the other person is wrong, we can think about the story and how both parties were looking at something from two different angles. Instead of arguing that he or she was right and that the other didn't know what he or she was talking about, they could have taken a moment to look at the situation from the other's point of view. If the mother and father had walked around the statue to see the shield from a different direction, each would have discovered they were both right. It was only the point of view from which they observed the statue that differed.

The children were wise in pointing out that the parents were both right in how they saw it but were both wrong in fighting so vehemently over it. The argument became so loud it disturbed the peace of the zoo.

This is what happens to us. We are so intent on proving ourselves right that we are ruining the peace of our own inner landscape. We fail to enjoy our inner peace because of the loud arguments playing out in our mind. We may be thinking negative things about others who have different points of view than we have. Or we may be verbally fighting with someone. Some may even succumb to physical blows.

What is more valuable to us in the long run—proving ourselves right or experiencing bliss and joy within? What do we gain by proving we are right and others wrong? A momentary victory for our ego? But if we learn to discuss differences calmly, taking time to understand the point of view of another, we will be the victorious winners. What we will gain is harmonious relationships.

When we develop our mind, we gain more understanding of others. We do not find a need to have intense arguments. Rather, we learn to discuss each situation calmly to find a solution. We don't rush to judgment but take time to hear the other person fully. We then try to stand in that person's shoes, walk around to see their side of the situation, and then weigh in from the other point of view. By looking at a problem from all sides, we come to a broader and better solution. We open our minds to other opinions or points of view. The other person is then likely to do the same and look at things from our point of view. Then, both can put their heads together to find the best solution in a calm, peaceful way.

Taking a lesson from the story, we can start looking at a situation from all sides. In this way, we can remain calm, cool, and collected. Stepping back from a situation, we can find many angles from which it can be viewed. Learning to navigate the many challenges of our relationships, we can maintain our equanimity.

Sweetness permeates our relationships when we learn how to detox our mind. By learning tools to navigate disagreements and arguments, we can find solutions to maintain our loving closeness. When we detox our mind, we can prevent heartache and pain from our relationships and instead enrich our lives with love and kindness.

Exercise: Reflect on relationship problems you may have had with members of your family, spouse, partner, loved one, co-workers, friends, and neighbors. Recall the pain and heartache you might have suffered from such difficulties. How would your life have been different if you had a way to prevent or overcome such problems and instead maintain a good relationship? Think about current relationship problems you may have and reflect on how your life would be happier and more peaceful if you had a technique or strategy to deal with them in a positive manner.

CHAPTER 7:

Live a Life of Peace and Joy

Detoxing the mind can improve our physical, mental, and emotional health. It can help us concentrate, be more efficient, productive, and successful at our academic studies, career, job, hobbies, or sports. A significant benefit of freeing our mind of toxins is living a life of peace.

When we boil down the goal of our physical and mental health and worldly endeavors, we find most people are striving to be happy. We feel good when our body is healthy and our mind is free of mental and emotional problems. We feel satisfied when we do well at our academic, work, or sports endeavors. Success brings with it a feeling of happiness. At their core, most people seek to feel joyful.

A shortcut to attaining happiness is to detox our mind. If we rid our mind of toxins, we would return to our natural state of peace and joy. Our original state is being a still pool that reflects the beauty of its natural surroundings, free of ripples.

If we reflect on moments in which we took a vacation and looked out at a still lake, at the clear blue sky, or a field of multi-colored flowers, we may have felt in touch with the peace within us—our true essence. Maybe we experienced those calm moments by looking at the grandeur of a mountain. Perhaps the sound of ocean waves against the beautiful sands of a beach brought us peace. We may recall a time and place in which we felt all the problems of the world melting away. In such moments, we may have felt in tune with our inner nature and the universe. Joy may have sprung from our hearts. Contentment and peace with the world may have bathed us. Such moments are mirrors into what our true nature is. We have at our essence a still center bubbling with joy. The only reason we are not aware of it is that we are wrapped up in the various toxins that pollute our mind.

Consider what happens when we travel in an airplane. As the plane taxis on the runway, we may be surrounded by fog, clouds, and a dark threatening sky about to burst forth with storms. However, when we lift off and the plane ascends to an altitude above the clouds, we soar into a blue sky and see the sun shining. We look down at the tops of billowy clouds. This is what happens when we detox the mind. We rise from the dark clouds of stormy thoughts to a clear, peaceful sky.

Once we learn to live in an attitude of detoxification, we can face the storms of life with calm. We can live in the still eye of a hurricane where tumultuous winds threaten everything around us, but we remain protected and safe in its calm center. Whether we face financial, career, health, or relationship problems, we are able to face them with fortitude and strength. By doing so, we do not add to the stress that devolves into health problems physically, mentally, or emotionally. We are able to still function in our studies, training, or work. We can remain calm at our center no matter what is happening around us.

Life is filled with problems. There have always been difficulties and there will always be challenges. That is a given for all human beings. It is how we deal with them that makes the difference between someone who can stay positive and happy and someone who succumbs to sadness. We can feel the sorrows of life, but it does not disturb the equanimity at our core.

To illustrate this, there is a story of a father who was doing some repairs to his house. His young son watched to see what his father was doing. Growing interested, the boy wanted to learn how to do the carpentry work alongside his father.

The father showed him how to measure and cut wood. He taught him how to remove old pieces to replace with new ones. They worked hard for a long time.

Then, the father showed his son how to hammer a nail into the wood. For a while they put pieces of wood together, hammering the nails in the wood. They then became fatigued. When the boy lifted the hammer to strike another nail, he was not paying attention. Missing the nail, the boy hit his own finger.

Hitting it so hard the boy screamed out. He jumped up to rush into the house for ice.

The father looked up and saw what had happened.

When the father realized no one was in the house to get ice for the boy, he leapt to his feet to rush in to help his son. The boy was screaming in great pain.

The father got the ice, but the boy was in too much pain to calm down to let his father put the ice on him. The boy thought that putting freezing ice on a wound was painful and he resisted.

Not knowing what he could do to help his son, he had an idea. He took a bowl, filled it with water, and put the ice in the bowl to chill the water. The boy still resisted putting his hand into the icy water.

Finally, the father said, "Will you put your hand in if I put mine in with it?" The man took the boy's hands and together they dipped their hand into the water. This calmed the boy down. As they sat together with both of their hands in the water, the boy calmed down.

Every few minutes they would remove their hands from the water to let the feeling return to their hands, and then dip it again. They continued like this for a number of minutes until the boy began to feel better.

Turning to his father, the boy said, "I am glad you are here with me."

The story illustrates that the boy had to go through a painful experience, but the comforting presence of his father softened it. The pain may be there, but the comfort and peace of protection lessen the suffering. We too can derive comfort from the peace within us even when faced with life's challenges.

If we could detox our mind, our life would be filled with happiness, peace, and joy.

Exercise: Recall times in your life when you experienced peace and joy. Was there a special place that put you into that state? Did you have an experience that brought you into that happy frame of mind? Imagine that you could be in that state whenever you wanted. Think about how reverting into that state of joy and calm could keep you out of the stress and pain that life's challenges bring. Pick a challenge in your life where toxins threaten to bring you down. Instead, shift your attention into that state of happiness you remember. See how it helps you deal with your difficulties in life by keeping your from sinking into the mental toxins that deprive you of your natural state of happiness.

CHAPTER 8:

The Wonders of Spiritual Health

One of the greatest benefits of detoxing your mind is for your spiritual health. While seeking happiness in this world, the realization dawns on each person at some point in life that everything of this world that is material in nature is not lasting. While occupied with daily life, we remain absorbed only in the outer world. We are busy taking care of our body, our family, our house, our belongings, and going to school or a job to have a career to support us. Beyond basic survival, we also seek happiness in a variety of pastimes, whether physical, mental, or emotional. But whenever faced with challenges, we question whether we can really be truly happy when we can lose all that we rely on for happiness.

When we suffer the loss of our health, finances, possessions, or loved ones, the pain and suffering is enormous. We realize there is nothing in this world that is lasting. Everything made of matter decays, including our own bodies. The moment we awake to the fact that we are mortal and our life span is limited, we may begin to question what is our purpose in life, why are we here, and do we exist beyond this physical life. This awareness is often termed as our moment of spiritual awakening. We start to seek a happiness that will outlast matter, outlast our material world, and outlast our physical existence. The panic that accompanies loss drowns us in a sea of sadness. It saps the joy of life. It can so occupy our attention, that we may struggle with our daily existence.

Benefits to Our Spiritual Health by Detoxing Our Mind

When we detox our mind, we find a still center of calm within us. What we are tapping into is our true nature, our spiritual essence. The peace we feel within is not only attributed to the absence of outer problems; that inner happiness is the state of our spirit, which is who we truly are.

When someone is drowning in the ocean, turbulent waves may swirl around the person. But when a lifeline is thrown in, the person can be pulled safely from the raging sea. Similarly, the storms of life are buffeting us here, there, and everywhere. But if we take hold of the lifeline within us, we are safe and at peace. Within us is a spark of happiness that is our true essence. It is there all the time. When we detox our mind, we then can take sanctuary in that still center, permeating us with lasting happiness and peace.

Spiritual health means tapping into the love and joy that exists within us. It is our essential core that is not made of matter; it is ethereal, transcendent spirit that outlasts our physical body. This is our immortal self that lasts beyond this body and even the physical universe. It was always there and will always be there. By identifying with our inner core, we touch immortality. This inner self is an eternal ball of consciousness. When we detox our mind, and clear away the poisons that pollute our attention, we find its still, tranquil center of joy.

Tapping into our spiritual center gives us a new perspective on life. We can deal with life's problems in a calmer, more balanced way. We may still encounter problems, but we have a place of retreat within us to fill us with calm anytime we want. It is like carrying within us a spa retreat in which we can relax and enjoy anywhere. It does not cost anything to visit it. We can tap into it whether at home or on the road. We can take a dip into the waters of that spa for as long as we want any time of day. It is available 24/7 and never closes. By tapping into it, we are boosting our spiritual health. The by-product of spiritual health is lasting spiritual love. It is ours when we detox our mind.

Exercise: **Throughout your life, remember and jot down times that you had moments when you questioned your purpose in life, why are you here, and if there is anything beyond this physical life? If so, recall a time that your longing to know the answers to these mysteries was most intense. Now picture a pool within you where you can dive in to learn the answers. If you were told you could** access these answers if you cleared the toxins from your mind, reflect on whether you would want to learn the steps to do so.

CHAPTER 9:

Attain Spiritual Enlightenment

Boosting our spiritual health has multiple benefits. Bathing in a pool of peace and calm within can help us deal with life's problems. Yet even more wondrous gifts await us when we tap inside.

When we visit a spa and dip our feet into a warm pool, that is the only part of us that feels its soothing waters. But if we were to dive in completely, our whole body would feel the relaxation of the waters wash over us. Similarly, when we detox our mind, we initially feel mentally peaceful. However, when we immerse ourselves more fully into a state where our mind is purified of toxins, our whole being would experience bliss. When completely focused within, we can attain spiritual enlightenment.

The bar to achieving spiritual awareness is our absorption into our mental toxins. For example, consider the effects of pollution in this world. Toxic wastes sully our rivers, lakes, and oceans. Our air is polluted by emissions from vehicles, toxins spewing from manufacturing plants, and forest fires burning throughout the world. Few dare to drink polluted water. We may have experienced physical difficulties with our breathing, due to asthma, allergies, or burning eyes from air pollution. Just as outer pollution prevents us from drinking clean water and breathing fresh air, so do mental toxins pollute us from enjoying the wonders of spiritual treasures within.

The Benefits of Detoxing Our Mind to Attain Spiritual Health

Streams of higher consciousness in the form of inner Light and Sound flow constantly within us. A brief encounter with our still center is the start of a journey on this stream of Light and Sound leading to wondrous discoveries within. Flowing on this inner stream to higher states of consciousness fill us with spiritual love and ecstasy. We tap into the immortal side of our self not restricted by the limitations of this physical world.

When the ripples of the pool cease, we can see into eternity. Spiritual Light and celestial Music reverberates. It is more than just an experience of our outer eyes and ears. There is an inner Light and Sound that pulsates with consciousness, uplifting love, unending happiness, and joy. When immersed in this experience, our whole being is uplifted into states of ecstasy. The more absorbed we become into the Light and Sound, we transcend to realms of beauty and bliss beyond what we experience in this physical universe. These realms are filled with colors and music beyond any known in this world. We realize that there is more to our existence than our body and mind and this physical world. We identify with our inner self, as soul. The soul itself is all consciousness, all Light, all celestial Music, and all love and bliss.

What would that mean for our life if we had an inner source of peace, love, and bliss to tap into anytime we want? Each time we access it, our consciousness could be elevated to connect with wisdom, connectedness, and immortality.

Exercise: **Imagine what it would mean for you to see for yourself realms of beauty and bliss within. Then, picture yourself accessing this inner treasure anytime you want. Would you rather spend time drowning in the mental toxins to which you have been habituated to focus on, or would you rather bathe in an eternal ocean of lasting peace and joy? If you could have the keys to remove the pollution of your mind to experience the wonders of your natural inner state, reflect on whether you would want to use them.**

PART 3:

Personal Improvement Plan to Detox Your Mind

CHAPTER 10:

Personal Improvement Plan: Meditation Instructions

Part 1 of this book described how detoxification applies not only to ridding our body of toxins that prevent us from good health, but how detoxing our mind leads to a life of peace and happiness. An array of mental toxins were presented to make us aware of the ones we want to eliminate for a more joyful life

Part 2 delineates the multiple benefits that can be ours when we detox our mind. Keeping our mind clear of toxins can boost our physical, mental, and emotional health, improve our relationships, help us achieve academic, job, career, or sports success, and attain spiritual health and enlightenment.

In Part 3 we will learn a simple, effective meditation technique as part of our personal improvement plan to detox our mind. We will explore various categories of toxins that plague us and gain practical strategies and methods for detoxing our mind for a life of happiness and peace. The exercises can help us reflect on the effect toxins have had on our lives so far and engage us in actively reducing them. While going through this chapter, note toxins that prevent you from a life of happiness and peace. Then, select the strategies and exercises you plan to try to eliminate those toxins.

Meditation as a Safe, Natural Method for Detoxing Our Mind

The technique of meditation is safe and natural. One can practice it anytime and at any place. Meditation is accessible 24/7 as the Light and Sound current reverberates within each person.

The practice involves sitting still comfortably, closing one's eyes, and focusing one's attention within. There is no difficult physical poses or positions one must take. It can be done by anyone, whether healthy or infirmed, as it does not require any physical strength or agility to do it. For those who cannot sit due to a physical problem, one can meditate lying down. However, unless there is a physical reason to do so, it is not encouraged because it may lead to falling asleep, and we need to be awake to meditate.

Meditation can be performed as an experiment in which we test the practice to see the benefit for ourself. Every moment bathed in the inner Light and Sound cleanses our mind of the toxins that make us unhappy. We emerge from meditation with a sense of joyousness. Inner intoxication bubbles within. Connecting with the inner Light and Sound in meditation leads to states of ecstasy.

The cleansing effect of meditation washes away the toxins that distract our mind. In earlier chapters, we looked at all the obstacles that toxins place on our physical and mental health, our performance in our worldly tasks, and our relationships with others. We saw the devastating effects these toxins have on us. We can find tranquility through the detoxifying benefits of meditation on the inner Light and Sound.

Meditation Technique: SOS Meditation on Inner Light and Sound

SOS Meditation on the inner Light and Sound is an easy method suitable for modern times. We can practice it in the comfort of our homes, on a break at work, or any place we choose. People of all backgrounds, cultures, or ages can do it. One can make the practice a part of one's life without having to leave one's home to meditate in a cave, mountaintop, or jungle. We can make it a part of whatever lifestyle we are leading.

In this scientific age, people no longer want to go on blind belief or hearsay. They want to experience for one's self with one's own eyes. Thus, meditation on inner Light and Sound can be practiced as a science where one tests the hypothesis to experience the results.

When we test the hypothesis of meditation on the inner Light and Sound, we can experience dramatic benefits. No one could have convinced us of the experiences that meditation brings until we practice it. This is why it is important to do the experiment within the laboratory of our own body to see whether meditation can really detox our mind and bring lasting peace and happiness.

Instructions for SOS Introductory Meditation on Light

The SOS Meditation on the inner Light and Sound leads to firsthand experience of the glorious treasures within us. To get started, we can try on our own the introductory SOS Meditation technique to begin the process of detoxing our mind on our road to peace and joy.

In SOS Meditation, we sit in a comfortable pose, most convenient to us, in which we can sit still for the longest possible time. While meditating, we do not hold hands or touch anyone else, as any movement brings our attention back down into the body. This would distract us from concentration on the seat of the soul, located between and behind the two eyebrows.

We close our eyes, gently, as we do when we go to sleep, but we remain wide awake. Closing our eyes keeps us from being distracted by the outer sights of the physical world. With closed eyes, we focus our attention in front of us. We do not put pressure on our eyes. We also do not raise our eyes upwards towards the direction of the eyebrows as that puts pressure on our eyes and forehead and can result in a headache. Rather, we keep our eyes focused gently in front of us and look into the middle of what appears within. We keep gazing horizontally, focusing about eight to ten inches in front of us with closed eyes.

We look lovingly into the middle of what appears in front of us. We may at first see either darkness or light, sparks of light, pinpoints of light, flashes of light, circles of light, or light of any color, such as red, orange, yellow, blue, green, purple, violet, white, or a golden color. We should continue gazing into the middle of what appears. We may see inner vistas such as an inner sky, clouds, stars, a moon, or a sun.

While looking into the middle of what appears, we may notice that our mind sends thoughts that distract us from gazing within. We may find that we cannot silence our mind to continue meditating. To help keep our mind from distracting us, we can mentally and silently repeat any word that makes us feel peaceful. This repetition should go on mentally, and not out loud, as we continue to gaze. By gazing deeper into the middle of the Light, we can tap into the spiritual treasures within and enjoy profound peace, bliss, and happiness unlike any we have found in this world. Divine love engulfs and fulfills us. The beauty of meditation is that this joy remains with us even after we resume our daily activities.

Exercise: You can try this SOS Meditation technique at home and note its effects on you. Do you notice any physiological changes like slower breathing and heart rate? Do you feel calmer? Does physical, mental, or emotional stress decrease? Do you feel peace and happiness? Note its effects if you try it for some time each day.

CHAPTER 11:

Attaining Peace through Nonviolence

One group of toxins that harms our mind arises from violence. The root cause of violence is anger and hatred. When we suffer from angry or hateful thoughts it affects what we say and do. Anger and hatred lead to violent thoughts, hurtful criticism, intolerance, bigotry, and prejudice.

If we cleanse ourselves from the toxin of anger and hate in our mind, we can lessen and eliminate violence in our words and actions.

In this chapter, we will explore what each of the toxins associated with anger and hatred are and how they affect us. We can identify which ones we want to eliminate from our lives. Then, the rest of the chapter provides solutions to detox our mind from anger and hatred.

Anger

Anger arises when:
- we don't get what we want because someone or something is blocking us,
- we don't like what's happening to us, or
- things are not going the way we expected them to happen.

Anger can be directed towards people, inanimate objects, nature, life, or ourselves. For example, sometimes we become mad at objects that break or do not work properly. Bad weather that upsets our plans can frustrate us. We may grow angry at life for having to endure physical discomfort. Most of the time our anger is related to other people not giving us what we want, not agreeing with us, or causing us difficulties. There are times we are angry at one person but when we cannot express it, we take out our anger at someone else as an innocent bystander.

When toxins of anger or hatred reach a critical mass, some people resort to violent thoughts. They start thinking about hurting others. This is dangerous because the next step can lead toward violent words. One more step can result in violent deeds. When we wish others harm, we are on dangerous ground. This is the precarious step which is a precursor to violent words or actions. We have seen the tragic effect of violence in history.

What happens when we are angry? Anger triggers reactions within us that affect our mind and body. Our mind sends signals to the body to activate our fight or flight hormones. When faced with a danger that could threaten our lives, these hormones, such as adrenaline and cortisol, are released to give us the energy to either run from a predator or fight. These circulating hormones make our heart race, our muscles contract in preparation for running or fighting, and our breathing rate escalate. We may not take physical action by running or striking back, but our mind experiences distress as we try to overcome or escape our "enemy." We are in a state of mental disturbance and we try to find ways to fight back, whether by raising our voice, saying hurtful things, or plotting revenge against the person.

Why does the body release these hormones when not facing real danger to our life? The original purpose of these hormones was to help us survive. Useful when faced with a truly life-threatening situation, these hormones can become harmful when released frequently or for long periods for only lesser threats. In daily life, we take as threats simple events such as someone criticizing us or not giving us what we believe is rightfully ours. We may even become irate if someone in our household leaves off a cap from the toothpaste tube. Because we can't control our anger, our temper rises. Soon adrenaline and cortisol are rushing to protect us just as it would do if our life depended upon it. Where then has our peace of mind gone? We cannot find rest unless we "conquer" the person or situation causing us this distress.

One of three things may happen:

1) we react towards others and set in place a cycle in which they then react to us, and that cycle continues; or
2) we cannot let it go and we fall deeper and deeper into a pit of anger and revenge that we can't climb out of; or
3) we realize we have gotten ourselves worked up over nothing, we let it go, and calm down.

A question to ask is, "Who does anger hurt?" In this

connection, there is an example from the life of Lord Buddha. One day, he was sitting with his disciples when a person approached who did not believe in the Buddha's teachings and wanted to discredit him. The agitated person began calling the Buddha many names and speaking ill of him.

Buddha's disciples immediately reacted and wanted to punish the man for him speaking so disrespectfully to their teacher.

However, Buddha stopped them and said, "Do not harm him."

Then, Buddha, turned to the man and said, "Dear friend, this gift of anger that you brought I do not accept." The man turned and left.

When the disciples inquired of Buddha as to why he responded in such a way, the Enlightened One said, "If I do not accept his gift of anger, with whom is the gift left?"

Buddha was letting them know that if we do not accept the anger sent to us, it stays or returns to the sender. Thus, if we have angry thoughts about someone, the anger stays in our system and we are the ones who are hurt.

Science and medicine are now illustrating this principle. Researchers can observe the biological reaction that takes place in our brain and our body when under stress or filled with anger. They study how anger sets off a chain reaction in the body in which certain hormones are released. The hormones activate specific responses in the body. While these hormones direct the body to run or fight to save itself, without a physical threat we internalize the anger. Since we do not need to run or fight, those hormones merely circulate in our body, causing unnecessary stress to our cells and organs. Doctors have correlated this response to development of stress-related ailments. Thus, people over time are at risk for problems such as high blood pressure, heart disease, stroke, breathing problems, difficulty with skin conditions, and other ailments. Medical research thus sheds light on the fact that anger hurts the sender. Our angry thoughts cause a physiological reaction, which can cause damage to our health.

These hormones circulating through us activated by anger can lead to physical health problems and stress-related illnesses. They can also lead to a host of secondary mental thoughts that create even more difficulties for us. Our mind is no longer at peace but ruminates over the anger we feel and the blame we place on others who we believe "caused" us to get angry. The truth is, no one can cause us anger unless we ourselves allow them to make us angry.

Exercise: Note down times you were angry and what physical and mental reactions it caused you. How did anger affect your peace of mind?

Criticism

When someone does something we do not like, we may start to criticize him or her. We may think, "Why did he do that? Why did she do the work that way? Why is he making mistakes when he should know better? Why is she talking like that?" The list goes on and on. What happens to our peace of mind?

Criticism arises when we don't agree with the words or deeds of others. We become observant of what they do and make comments about their words, actions, or decisions. When we leave that person, we review all the faults we observed. We may even talk about their failures with others. Think of how much time we spend thinking and talking about others.

Video replays on our televisions, computers, or digital devices allow us to replay any show or program. When we watch a replay of something already viewed, it takes the same amount of time to watch it again. We end up spending double the time on the original action. This is what happens when we criticize others. We observed what they did once, but then replay it in our mind to criticize every step of what was done.

We lose valuable time that our mind could use for other more helpful activities. Instead of wasting time replaying areas of disagreement on what others do, we could use the time productively on our jobs to improve or develop new ideas or processes. It can be applied to learning a new skill at school or work. We can use the time to be physically fit. It could be used to deepen our relationships with our loved ones. We can also use our precious time to develop spiritually. If we spent time in self-improvement instead of criticizing others, we'd gain greater benefits.

If we could detox our mind from criticizing others, we'd be more peaceful and blissful.

Exercise: Note times you criticized others. How could you have used that time to be more peaceful or improve your own self?

Violent Thoughts

We consider that the dark ages of the past are over. We read in history of the brutality of humans toward each other and think, "I'm glad those days are gone." However, a peek at the news, either in the newspaper or on the Internet, social media, or TV reveals that violence still plagues our planet. Violent thoughts persist.

Why do people harbor thoughts of hurting others? The causes are many, but the results are the same. We are angry when things don't go our way. Someone hurts us, and we want to retaliate. We desire to gain something that others have, and we are not successful in attaining it. When people have angry thoughts or visualize hurting someone, they enter the realm of violence. In this way, our mind is filled with the toxins of violent thoughts.

Many people have passing angry thoughts, but their conscience tells them it is wrong, so they never convert those thoughts into actions. They take control over their thoughts. If they realize a thought is violent and if acted upon it can harm others, they do not convert thought into action. However, if not taught self-control, some may act on their violent thoughts, bringing pain to others and themselves.

By detoxing our mind we can wash away the poisons that percolate in our mind related to violence. As long as these toxic violent thoughts rush through our mind, we are not at peace. Violent thoughts feed on themselves and escalate which can lead to our planning and scheming on how to hurt someone. Soon, our mind is engaged in intricate plans to put these violent thoughts into action. Our mind is poisoned, and we risk spreading that to others when we act on it.

Detoxing the mind includes ridding ourselves of violent thoughts. By doing so, our mind will be calm and peaceful. When someone does something we don't like, instead of getting even we should choose to remain calm.

Exercise: List times that you recall having violent thoughts towards others. Did those thoughts arise many times? Reflect on how these thoughts affect your own peace.

Solutions for Detoxing Ourselves from Anger through Nonviolence

Simple techniques can eliminate the toxins of violence and replace them with the soothing balm of nonviolence.

Meditation offers a safety net from falling into violence. How can meditation be so powerful?

When we meditate on the inner Light and Sound, we gain an angle of vision in which we see how the Light within connects all as one family. When we recognize that the Light in us is also in all others, we see all as one human family, even if deeply flawed. Within a family, members love and help each other. Even if there are disagreements, there is a basic love and a sense of caring within that family. No one purposely wants to bring harm to others.

When we recognize that all human beings are part of one family, we can extend our care and love to encompass everybody. With this angle of vision, we can reduce our violent thoughts. We may disagree with others or have different points of view, but do not let them escalate to thoughts of harming anyone. We don't think of being violent with anyone. Meditation on the inner Light and Sound replaces violent thoughts with nonviolence and thoughts of love and concern for others.

Meditation on the inner Light and Sound can detox our mind from the poison of anger. When immersed in the pool of Light and Sound within, outer irritants of life are washed away. We are then bathed with inner contentment. We feel good so that whatever made us angry no longer bothers us. Think about how a child has a tantrum when you take his or her lollipop away. Yet replace it with a favorite ice cream, then the child quickly forgets the lollipop. Similarly, if we replace whatever it is that we did not receive with a far greater source of happiness, our anger can subside. By meditating on the Light and Sound we are filled from within with happiness. We can experience such joy that we may even ask, "What was making me angry before? I don't even remember what it was."

Once, Mother Teresa was asked by someone, "Do you ever become angry by all the examples of social injustice that you see around you in India and in other parts of the world in which you work?"

Mother Teresa beautifully answered, "Why should I expend energy in anger when I can expend it in love?"

Mother Teresa's comment illustrates a high angle of vision from which we can lead our lives. As we go through our lives, we come across many situations that can provoke anger. To overcome anger, we can stay calm in face of whatever is happening to us. As we face problems at home, in our office, or driving in traffic, we should not react. We can recognize that difficulties are there but take steps to solve the problem. We can be proactive and try to remove the agitating source through communication or finding peaceful solutions. Anger is not going to eliminate problems. All that it will do is make our own blood pressure go up, cause fight or flight hormones to circulate through our body and make us ill. Our anger does not cause the others to stop doing what they are doing. All anger does is to make us ineffective. But if we remain calm, we can tackle the problem with all our faculties fully in our control.

What steps can we take to overcome anger? First, when we feel ourselves getting angry, we should not say or do anything immediately. Rather, we should take a deep breath and slow down. Then, we should sit in meditation. We should remove ourselves from the situation to be alone and sit in a state of meditation. If angry thoughts try to intervene, we should ask ourselves whether we want to make the spirit of anger stronger. If we wish to be calm, we can do so by not feeding the spirit of anger. We should realize that the longer we can remain calm, quiet, and composed, the less energy our anger will have. It will gradually vanish.

We can follow the example of Abraham Lincoln who, during the Civil War, when he was accused of being friendly to the enemy, he said, "Don't I destroy my enemies when I make them my friends?"

We can destroy anger by our equipoise and balance. While the situations that incite us continue, we do not want to become bound to them. We want calmly to pass through them. We can use our energy for more constructive purposes and be peaceful.

One cause of anger is relationship problems. Parents struggle to get along with their children. Children feel their parents are challenging. Spouses or people living with their significant others find cause for disagreements. Co-workers, friends, and neighbors find causes for strife. The discomfort we feel when not getting along with another person can be so great, we become too preoccupied in figuring out how to resolve our problem. For those trying to focus on meditation and higher aspects of life, relationship problems can pose a barrier as it occupies our attention.

What is the secret to a happy relationship to bring us peace? In this connection, there is the story of two co-workers who decided to go into business together. They worked hard building their business which over time proved successful. When they had been in business for forty years, they held a celebration. In modern times, when many businesses or relationships between two partners don't last, it was remarkable that they had stayed together for so many years.

They held a banquet and invited their family, friends, clients, and associates to celebrate the forty-year anniversary of their business partnership.

On the day of the party, their guests showed up to celebrate the two. Festivities included music and delicious food.

As they all sat down to dinner, one of the friends raised a glass to make a toast. He said, "So few people make it to forty years of staying partners in a business." The guests admired how long these two men had stayed together in business without having a fight and going separate ways. They asked what their secret was to stay in a business partnership together for such a long time.

The two men looked at each other and whispered to each other for a few moments.

One of them stood up and said, "In all the years we spent together, we had not fought with each other even once."

The guests looked at each other in astonishment and whispered amongst them.

One of their other friends, who knew them well, called out in fun, "We know both of you. We know how argumentative and critical you can be. Do you really expect us to believe that?"

The other man confirmed what the first had said, "Yes, it's true."

One of their other friends stood and said, "Come on, how can we believe that? You have such a hot temper. You get upset at the slightest thing."

One of the friends of the other partner said, "And I can say the same thing about my friend. He has such an angry temper. How can we expect to believe that the two of you never fight?"

The two partners looked at each other and whispered a few more things in each other ears.

One of them gestured for the other to provide the answer.

He said, "You are right. We both have angry tempers. We get mad at the smallest things in life."

The one making the toast then asked, "So how is it you stayed in business together for so long and claimed not to have ever had a fight?"

One of the men replied, "Here is the secret to our happy relationship."

Every guest perked up and sat up at the edge of the seat, eager to hear the answer.

The man continued, "When we went into partnership, we made a special pact. Would you all like to know what that was?"

The guests all called out "yes," as they wanted to know.

The man said, "We made a pact with each other that the two of us would never lose our temper at the same time. We promised that if one of us became angry, the other would remain patient. If only one is complaining or fighting, but the other is silent, there is no quarrel. It is one-sided. Because we kept this agreement for all the forty years we've been in business, we never had a fight. It takes two to fight. With one person, it is not a fight. This has been the secret of our happy work relationship all these years."

Think about how deep the meaning is for our own lives. A fight involves two people going back and forth hurling harsh words, complaints, and criticisms on each other. One person says something unkind, and the other responds with more critical words. Then, the first one replies, and back and forth it goes, on and on and on. Finally, after minutes, hours, days, and even weeks and months, the caravan of harsh words continues until the two don't even remember the initial disagreement they had.

However, if only one person expresses anger, and the other keeps mum, the complaining one gets it out of his or her system. With no reaction from the other, but a smile and patience, there is nothing more to be said. The burning flames of anger eventually die out.

If only one of them is talking and the other is silent, the sum total is that there is no argument. Without an argument, there is quiet which is a step toward an inner stillness needed to connect with God.

This formula for a happy relationship can be put to a test in any of our relationships. We can use it when dealing with our children who are complaining and throwing a tantrum when they don't get their way. Children can use it with their parents who are not happy with something they are doing. Co-workers can use it at work when they are about to fight over a policy or a work situation. Spouses, or those in relationship with each other, can use it each time they are about to have a fight over something. Most of the time people in families fight over trivial things, like leaving the cap off toothpaste, or who is right and who is wrong on a question. They may fight about bigger things like how to spend their money or about making a decision on what house to buy. When a difference of opinion grows into a fight, then use the secret that only one is angry at one time and the other stays calm, cool, and collected. When the anger of the first one dies down, and things have cooled off, then the other may offer a point of view. If the second person cannot control himself or herself, and escalates into anger, then the other person can then stay quiet until the storm passes.

Situations in which we experience good results from acting calmly reinforce positive behavior. Situations in which we experience negativity from making bad choices provide opportunities to learn by figuring out how to overcome the situation. We can choose to behave angrily and then observe whether a tough situation grows worse. Or we can choose to act with nonviolence and learn how to diffuse a negative situation.

Having relationship problems is an opportunity to learn to become a better person to grow. If we are beset with anger, then it means we must learn the lesson of nonviolence and patience. If we fail at this lesson, we may find that our relationships deteriorate. However, if we succeed in remaining calm, we will notice the problem dissipates. This forms a habit in which we learn how to act nonviolently the next time we are faced with a similar situation.

The statement, "Rome was not built in a day," reminds us that it takes many repetitions of a lesson for it to be learned. We may fail at being angry hundreds or even thousands of times, but if we keep trying to be patient with those who are angry with us, a day will come when we will master the lesson. We will remain calm when attacked by someone's anger. The peace we experience will be so delightful, we won't want to revert to our old negative behaviors of the past.

Introspection is a method that helps to observe how we act when faced with someone else's temper. If we focus on developing nonviolence and patience, we can note how many times a day we react negatively in response to someone's anger. We can then resolve to lessen our reaction by one angry moment less each day. Over time we will reduce our reactions from hundreds to dozens, and then to even single digits. Ultimately, we will be like the two business partners in the story who were able to declare that they never had an argument. We too will be able to refrain from reacting to another's anger.

Sometimes when we remain calm, others develop admiration for us. For example, they notice how upset they always are, while they see us as always calm and balanced. Others may reach a point where they get sick and tired of fighting. They may realize that their angry monologues are met with silence so they finally give up. When they find no reaction from us to their angry tirades, they may stop throwing tantrums and turn peaceful. Then both sides may eventually learn to peacefully have differences without them escalating into fights.

Those who learn meditation have an extra tool to use against anger. When someone is upset with us, whether a family member, such as a spouse, parent, or child, or a friend, co-worker, or anyone else, meditation helps us stay calm. As soon as the onslaught from the other person ends, we can sit in meditation. That will help us stay patient. The other person may have hurled onslaughts of words at us, but we focus on the peace within.

Through meditation, we contact a source of happiness within us. The joy we experience inside stays with us even when we come out of meditation. This lasts throughout the day. We are able to handle the difficulties in a balanced state. Over time, our equanimity brings a calming effect on our environment.

By making a pact with others to only have one person angry at a time, coupled with meditation, we too can learn the secret to a happy relationship. By practicing this we will start a new habit, where we can even eliminate the thoughts of anger towards others and detox our mind.

Replace Revenge with Sweet Forgiveness

Conflicts, violence, and wars around the world cause tremendous suffering. One cause of violence stems from the desire for revenge. Someone hurts us, so we seek to hurt them back. Then, they retaliate. We react by paying them back for the pain they caused us. A cycle of violence, either in thought, word, or deed begins. Some cycles of revenge may last for days, weeks, months, years, and in some cases centuries.

How can we ever have a world of peace if the cycle of vengeful retaliation does not end? Is there any cure for the toxin of revenge? The solution for ending a cycle of vengefulness is within us. An antidote to the toxin of revenge lies in developing forgiveness.

There is a beautiful story about Clara Barton, who founded the nursing profession. She was a forgiving person and never held any grudge or resentment toward anyone. One day a friend reminded Clara of a wrong the friend had done to Clara many years earlier and wanted to apologize for what she had done. Clara would not even recall what the incident was for which the person was apologizing. When the person said, "Don't you remember the wrong I had done to you?" Clara lovingly replied, "No, I distinctly remember forgetting that!"

If we can be like Clara and purposely forget the wrong, our mind and heart will be clear. When we forgive and forget we are letting go of the past. We are saying, "I forgive the person for what has happened. Then I am going to forget about it." We are letting it go. When we can let go of the past wrongs done by others, the gain is that we detox our mind. This leaves our mind clear to drink from the fountain of peace bubbling from within. Waves of bliss await us, but to experience it we need our mind to be clear of all anger. Cleansing our heart and mind of the toxin of revenge opens us up to happiness.

The cycle of vengeance can end through the power of sweet forgiveness. Harboring a desire for revenge when someone has wronged us poses a great challenge towards attaining peace in this world. It is easy to be peaceful when everything is going one's way. However, when someone hurts us, it takes

strength to withhold one's anger and not lash out at the perpetrator. The need to take revenge on those who hurt us leads to
a vicious cycle of retaliation.

There are two roads each of us has a choice to take. When
someone injures us in word or deed, we can choose the path
of revenge and retaliation, or we can choose the path of
forgiveness. For those who choose the path of revenge there
is no end to the retaliation. Each person returns tit for tat
which can last for days, months, or years. If we look at history,
we find this vengeance causing wars for centuries. It takes
courage to stop the cycle of revenge and instead choose the
path of forgiveness. Forgiveness washes away the hurts of the
past and replaces them with human kindness.

To detox our mind from revenge we make the choice that if
someone hurts us, we can forgive. This will preserve our own
peace and will not escalate into a larger battle. Replacing the
sorrows of the world with kindness will cause the hearts of
others to blossom. In return, our own heart will bloom with
flowers of love.

If we forgive, we maintain thoughts, words, and deeds of
goodness. We have seen cases in which a person who was
hurt did not respond. The result is that the one who brought
pain later regrets what he or she did because the recipient of
their hurt did not react. Instead, the hurt person continued to
act nonviolently to the perpetrator. Sometimes that person
regrets having hurt the other. Eventually the person who hurt
the other could be transformed. Without reacting, the calm
person serves as a mirror in which a hurtful person sees his
or her own reflection. When there is no reaction, the angry

person has a chance to calm down and see how foolish he or she had acted. That person may change his or her ways. The key is that we do not react negatively.

When weighted down by angry reactions, the energy of anger that we send out into the universe boomerangs back to us at some point. We wonder in life why we may be the victims of someone else's anger, but do not realize the possibility that it is only coming back to us from something we generated in the past.

Sometimes we respond with angry words. We see the effects verbal anger or abuse has on others. Wars are fought over words. Divorce courts are filled with cases of those who have decided to split up over words used against each other. Children grow up with psychological complexes over words their parents have spoken to them that were hurtful. When we are angry and send out hurtful words, it not only hurts the person to whom they are said, but like a boomerang, their effects come back to us at some point.

Even angry thoughts are potent. We think that no one knows what is going on in our heads, but that is not so. Thinking angry thoughts generate their own vibration. We send out vibrations into the atmosphere, and others can pick it up at a nonverbal level. We think no one knows what we are thinking, but they can sense that we have anger towards them. Raging thoughts may spill out with an angry tone of voice, even if we are saying something neutral or harmless.

Our angry thoughts may drive our actions. We make decisions based on our mental anger. Someone asks us to do something to help them, and in anger we say "no," when there is no reason that we should not help them. But our anger causes us to shun them.

When angry, we stand in the way of our own peace. How can we feel joy when our anger is in the way? We hear the expression, "Blinded with anger." Imagine that someone we care about comes to meet us lovingly and presents us with beautiful roses. Unfortunately, we are so wrapped up in our anger that we lash out at the person. We are blocking out the love that is coming our way by focusing on our anger.

We can rise above revenge by coming in contact with the peace within. If we each find inner peace, like a beacon it would radiate to all around us. Through a ripple effect, we could spread our own calm to the entire world.

As we are bathed in love, we are cleansed of the years of habits that caused us to have vengeful behaviors. We develop love, forgiveness, and compassion. This leads us to take the first step toward reconciliation and peace. Meditation can be incorporated into our everyday life.

In these troubled times, we can learn to meditate and find a place of calm and peace within. Every day we will be able to face the challenges of life. We will not only be peaceful ourselves, but we will radiate peace to all those with whom we come in contact. Peace begins with us. No one has ever been effective in trying to make others change and be peaceful. We can only change ourselves. By changing ourselves, we then become an example and have a positive effect on those who meet us. By seeing our kindness, others will be inspired to find out what has made our lives calm and peaceful. Then we can share with them that meditation has helped to transform us.

By transforming ourselves, we can transform others, including our family, community, society, and eventually the whole world.

As we experience the inner bliss and love, compassion and forgiveness flow from us toward those who have hurt us in the past. We build peaceful, harmonious, and loving relationships. In this way, we can rise above revenge and build a peaceful, safe world for ourselves and for posterity.

Exercise: Select helpful tips from this chapter to overcome any anger and then note if this makes you feel more peaceful.

CHAPTER 12:

Truthfulness:
A Life Free of Stress

Another set of poisons that keep us from being peaceful are lying, deceit, and hypocrisy. They stem from a lack of truthfulness. Lying, deceit, and hypocrisy means we are afraid to be who we really are. We want to think, act, and speak as if we were someone else. They represent different shades of deviating from truth.

Lying

Lying involves saying something different than what is fact or reality. When we lie, we must invent a story about a situation. We hide what really happened with some concocted information.

Then, we must keep the lie in our mind, so we consistently

tell people the same story. When we tell the truth, it's easy because we can refer back to the event and simply repeat it to others. But when we make up something, we must recall what we said to who and when. This takes mental energy.

After lying, we add worry to our toxins, because we are fearful that someone will find out it was not true. We become afraid of being caught changing a story we told. That causes others to doubt or mistrust us. This results in another set of other problems we must overcome when others stop trusting us.

Sometimes people are not truthful because they cannot face their own shortcomings, so they try to hide it not only from others but from themselves. They are not able to look themselves in the mirror to accept who they really are. Thus, they may lie to others while trying to hide the truth from themselves.

A lie begets worry and anxiety. We have laid a long road of mental poisons in our path. Lying is not just a one-time act. Lying infiltrates our mind, poisoning our peacefulness. Our peace of mind is disturbed not only at the time of telling a lie, but for a long winding road ahead.

Deceit

Another aspect of deviating from truth is deceit. Whereas a lie may focus on our words, deceit also can manifest as actions. It involves making people believe a situation is taking place when it really is not.

In society, people pretend to be what they are not. We may put on a big show to make ourselves appear better than what we are. We may be greedy but want to appear to others to be selfless. We may be an angry person but want to appear to others as being nonviolent. We may be ignorant but want to appear to be intelligent. We can deceive someone by acting as if we have a certain position in our company but really do not.

Deceit can become harmful when we take from others under a false pretense. Financial deceit, for example, is when we sell something to someone making them think it more valuable than it is, charge an unfair price, or sell something with no plans to deliver on it. A retailer can appear to be selling goods honestly but are secretly deceiving customers with inferior quality or inflated prices.

When the person we have cheated finds out, they lose trust in us. It is difficult to regain the trust of someone once it is lost. We have to work hard to regain that trust. People may look at us as if liars or cheats. Then, our word is no longer valued.

Deceit pollutes our mind. It causes us to plan out our deceit and keep a false story going in the minds of others. It takes much mental energy to deceive someone, hide something, and worry about being caught.

Being honest about who we are and what we do is easier than being deceitful. When we are honest, we earn the respect of others. Then, they will believe us because they know we have the virtue of truthfulness.

Hypocrisy

We pretend and make others believe that we are doing the right thing. In reality, we are doing what we accuse others of doing. We may see this in homes when a parent tells a teen not to drink alcohol or take intoxicating drugs, but the parent is doing it himself or herself. The child sees this hypocrisy and then tends to not believe the parent. The message to the child is to disobey what the parent says to do and instead follow the parents' examples, leading children to form bad habits.

We see those in authority telling everyone else how to behave but do not behave that way themselves. They make rules but break them themselves, creating a situation of distrust and noncompliance. Our mind fills with the toxin of hypocrisy when we are busy telling others what to do, but not practicing what we preach ourselves.

When we engage our mind into these poisons of lying, distrust, or hypocrisy, it disturbs our state of calm.

Exercise: Have you ever engaged in lying, deceit, or hypocrisy? If so, how much mental energy did it take to conceal the truth? How did such thoughts keep you from being peaceful?

Antidote of Truthfulness

Truthfulness means that we think, speak, and act in synchronicity with each other. If we think good thoughts, our words and deeds will be good. What is the use of thinking good thoughts, but having words and deeds that do not reflect that? Rather than speaking about how noble we are, it is better to live nobly. Better than speaking about how truthful we are, it is better to live truthfully. Better than speaking about how nonviolent we are, it is better to live nonviolently.

When we go to a doctor but hide from him or her our true symptoms, how can the doctor help us? The doctor cannot treat symptoms that he or she does not know about. We need to tell the doctor what we are feeling so the correct treatment can be administered.

Similarly, if we want to detox our mind from falsehoods such as lying, deceit, and hypocrisy, we can look objectively at ourselves. If we do not list our problems in this area, we cannot improve the next day. We can analyze ourselves and decide which habits we want to change.

Meditation can help us develop positive qualities. When we are in touch with a source of stability, peace, and happiness within ourselves, we become fearless and not afraid to be who we are. Then, we can live truthfully and not have to pretend who and what we are. We will be able to have positive qualities manifest in our lives in our thoughts, words, and deeds.

Be True to One's Self

Truthfulness is more than how we deal with people in our daily lives. It is more than telling the truth to our family, friends, or co-workers. Truthfulness also deals with our relationship with our inner self.

In this connection, there is an ancient tale about an emperor who was growing old. He did not have any children and began worrying about who would succeed him if he left this world.

He called his ministers to think about this problem. Finally, they posed to him a solution.

The next day the ministers bought him big sacks of seeds.

"Sir, we will take these seeds and roast them." After the ministers had them roasted, they put them into small bags to hold a few seeds each.

The king said, "This is an unusual plan. How will this help me find someone to inherit my empire?"

They told him, "You should send your messengers through all the land and announce that any young person, whether boy or girl, should come to your palace one week from today to meet with you." The king agreed but still did not understand how this would help him find an heir to his throne.

One week later, all the youth in the empire assembled in the courtyard in front of the palace.

The ministers told the king, "Announce to them that you are going to select one of them to be your emperor or empress."

When the king announced this to the crowd, the boys and girls cheered. How exciting to think that one of them could become the future emperor or empress of the land.

After the ministers told the king how to choose the winner the king explained to the crowd, "Each of you will receive a bag of seeds. To enter the competition, all you must do is grow flowers from them. The one with the most beautiful flowers from these special seeds will win."

The youths were happy that this was going to be easy to do. One by one they picked up a bag of seeds distributed by the emperor. They then left to go home to plant their seeds.

For several weeks they gave their seeds sunlight and watered them. But after a few weeks nothing grew. They each worried that they did not have the talent to grow flowers. But no one dared talk to anyone else lest the others would think they had failed. Each wanted to win so badly they did not want to tell anyone that they could not grow simple flowers. They were

CHAPTER 12: TRUTHFULNESS: A LIFE FREE OF STRESS

worried about being embarrassed and having the emperor think they were a failure.

When the announcement went through the empire that it was time to bring their flowers to the emperor, so he could judge which one grew the most beautiful ones, all the contestants in their own home felt embarrassed, ashamed, and disappointed that they could not win as they had no flowers.

When the day came to bring the flowers, a long line of teens formed in front of the emperor. Standing with the ministers, the emperor looked at what each had brought him. One by one, they presented a beautiful flower.

The king looked at the ministers, who also looked shocked.

"How is this possible?" the king asked his aides.

"We do not know, Sir."

Each of the teens had shown him a flower. The king looked disappointed.

The emperor took the ministers aside and asked, "I want someone with ethical qualities to inherit my throne so after me you will have a good leader. But look at each of these boys and girls. They lack virtue."

As the emperor was winding up the competition, a girl came running into the courtyard, breathless.

The king asked her to come forward. Approaching in humility she pulled out an empty flowerpot.

The king said, "Why are you coming with an empty flowerpot when I asked each to bring a flower so I could see which one was the most beautiful."

She said, "I tried my hardest to grow the seeds you gave me. I put them in the soil and gave them sunlight and daily water. But I am sorry to say, and please do not be mad at me, nothing grew."

The king smiled broadly and patted the girl on her head.

The king then asked all the young people assembled to sit.

He then said, "I am ready to announce the winner of the competition who will inherit my empire."

Everyone sat with anticipation, hoping it would be him or her.

The king said, "The winner is this girl who just arrived late."

Everyone went into an uproar, shouting and yelling.

"How can you pick her?" they all asked in unison. "She did not even grow a flower."

The king said, "Yes, that is why she has won. I purposely roasted the seeds so they would not sprout. I wanted to see which of you were honest enough to come empty-handed and explain that the seeds I gave you did not grow. But instead, you all tried to deceive and lie to me, bringing a flower from somewhere else as if grown by you from these seeds. She was the only one who tried to grow the flowers, and when it failed to grow, she had the virtue of telling me the truth. For this reason, she is the only one who showed the quality of truthfulness I want in the person who will carry on my work. The value of truthfulness is a noble virtue. For this reason, I will make her my successor."

This story clearly describes what happens when we engage in falsehood, which includes lies, deceit, or hypocrisy. When someone finds us out, they no longer trust us. We may at times feel we can get away with lying to others, but we cannot hide it from our inner self. If we can understand this simple fact, we would be more inclined to live our life with honesty, integrity, and a straightforward attitude.

Honesty Brings Peace

Through introspection we can see how much of our time is spent tracking or covering up our untruths. We can try to practice openness and honesty and then analyze whether it brings us closer to finding peace and happiness.

Once we recognize how we want to change, we can weed out our lapses. But if we are trying to hide what we thought, said, or did from our own self, then we cannot weed out our failures. We can only remove them when we recognize them and take steps to make changes. Then, these lapses can be eliminated. But if we even hide them from ourself, then how can we remove them? Honesty with our true selves has numerous rewards. When we recognize the ways in which we engage in the toxin of falsehood, we can work on removing them.

Meditation to Eliminate Toxins of Falsehood

One way to develop truthfulness is through meditation. The more we do so, we are in touch with the truth of our inner self. Our inner self lives in truth. It is the ego that plays the game of deceitfulness and untruth. The more we identify with the quality of truth, the calmer our life becomes.

In history, there is an example of practicing the virtue of truth. Mahatma Gandhi valued truthfulness. During one of his periods of nonviolent protest to help win independence for India he was arrested and put in jail. One of the rules of this particular jail stay was that prisoners were to receive no news-papers or news of the outside world.

One day, a doctor who was friendly with Gandhi Ji came to visit him in prison. He brought news that he thought Gandhi needed to know about how the nonviolent movement was doing. Knowing that the rules were that prisoners could not get news of the outside world, the doctor who had brought a newspaper, pulled out some of his papers and placed them on Gandhi's cot in his prison cell. The doctor proceeded to talk to Gandhi about his health and comforts. When it was time to leave, the doctor put all the papers from the cot back into his pocket, except he left the newspaper. He then departed.

When Gandhi saw the newspaper lying there, he refused to read it. In fact, he was so honest he did not want to break prison rules by even looking at it. Instead, Gandhi turned his back away from the newspaper on the bed and faced the corner of his cell the entire night. He sat up all night, with his face towards the corner so he would not see the newspaper or touch it.

The following morning, the doctor returned to visit Gandhi. Seeing the newspaper lying on the cot in the same place he had left it the previous night, the doctor asked, "I am sorry, but I left the newspaper here by mistake."

A smile crossed Mahatma Gandhi's face and Gandhi replied, "Yes, but you sentenced me to spend the whole night in a corner!"

Such was Gandhi's honesty that even if no one would see him read the paper, he did not want to be dishonest because he would know for himself that he broke the agreement he made to follow prison rules while there. How many of us live by such a degree of honesty?

What we do not realize is that we may hide what we do from others, but we cannot hide from our inner self. We have to live with the fruits of our actions. Our inner nature has the virtue of honesty. Whenever faced with a choice of being honest or dishonest, we can follow the dictates of either our soul or our ego. The ego leads us into many excuses to be dishonest. It has a thousand reasons why we should lie, cheat, steal, or deceive others. But our soul knows only honesty.

When we remove the toxins that pollute us, we identify with our soul. Is it worth denying ourselves peace and joy by telling a small lie or committing a dishonest act? The little money we may make by deceiving others or cheating others is not worth the delay we cause in attaining lasting peace and experiencing spiritual riches within. Those treasures are eternal and will stay with us permanently.

Truthfulness Is a Sign of Courage

Truthfulness means being in unison with one's thoughts, words, and deeds. Often, we think one thing but say another. Or we say one thing or do another. Or we think one thing and do another.

Lack of truthfulness involves fear. We fear something or someone, so we hide what we are really thinking. Our actions do not reflect our thoughts or our words. Sometimes it is our words that do not reflect our thoughts and actions.

When we are afraid, we need to find our courage. Lack of courage to stand up for what we believe causes us to hide.

Truthfulness is a sign of strength, while untruthfulness is a symptom of fear.

As we meditate and connect with our inner self we discover it is fearless. That inner essence is one with truth. We contact the Power that created all and is itself fearless. When we identify with that inner Power, we too become fearless. We then develop the courage to speak the truth and live truth. People will respect us and our words because they know we can be trusted. By developing the quality of truthfulness we will see positive changes in our lives.

We realize that when we are truthful, others respect us. Even if we honestly admit what we thought, did, or said to others, and it is not to their liking, or we admit a mistake, we gain their respect because we had the courage to speak up and admit our failure. That takes courage. They may not like what we did, but they respect that we were honest. In the end, many people will turn to us because they know we can be trusted.

When we say one thing but do another, we lose the trust of others. They no longer regard us with respect. Telling the truth is a quality of those who know they cannot hide from their true self. While feeling they may hide from others, they know who and what they are and that they cannot hide from themselves.

The following anecdote illustrates the value of truthfulness. There was a saint who was in the habit of arising at 4 o'clock each morning to sit in meditation. The saint had a horse that he would keep chained up at night in an open stable so that the horse would not run away, and no one could steal him.

One night, a thief snuck into the stable to steal the horse. He worked hard to untie the chains from the front. Then he

CHAPTER 12: TRUTHFULNESS: A LIFE FREE OF STRESS

discovered the horse was also chained in the rear. He set to work to untie the rear chains. But he found that the horse was tied from the front. He could not believe what he was seeing. Whenever he freed one set of chains from the front, the horse was chained in the back again. All night long he struggled to free the chains from both ends, but to no avail.

At four o'clock in the morning, the saint woke up and heard the commotion in the stable. He went outside and saw the man standing by his horse.

The saint said, "Who are you?"

The man recognized that he was stealing from someone known as a saint. Knowing that the saint knows everything replied in all openness, "I am a thief."

The saint said, "What are you doing here?"

The man said, "I have come to steal your horse. But this is strange. When I loosen the horse from the front side, it is chained from the back. When I undo the back chains, it is tied again from the front. This is so confusing. What is going on?"

The saint was amused and startled by the thief's honesty, openness, and frankness. The man did not make up any story about why he was here. He was frank about the fact that he had come to steal the horse.

The saint found it refreshing to meet someone who was honest. Most who came to him as disciples often hid the truth from him when he asked them questions. He wondered what kind of faith his disciples had if they did not even consider him to be all-knowing. If they thought they could deceive him, what kind of faith did they have in him and his oneness with the all-consciousness of the Creator? Yet, here was a man who was not even a disciple and was honest with him.

The saint said, "I am pleased with your honesty and your open confession. Due to your honesty, which I find quite refreshing, I will let you have the horse." The thief was grateful and appreciated the mercy and compassion of the saint. He vowed to give up his life as a thief and become a saintly man.

On the following day, some people from the village came to the saint.

The people told the saint, "We have lost our priest. We need a new priest. Can you suggest someone who leads an ethical life and could inspire us to also lead a godly life?"

The saint thought over all the people in the village and realized that no one had ethical qualities that would be a fit example for the congregation. At one time or another they had each been dishonest.

Finally, the saint said, "I have just the person for you." The saint called for the thief, who was resting in the stable with his new horse.

He turned to the people of the village and said, "He will be your new priest. He is the most honest man I met and can inspire the rest of you to be honest." The saint then sent the thief on the horse to the village to take over as the new priest.

This story illustrates that even though the thief was certainly unethical in that he was taking from others, that at the heart of hearts, at least he was honest about who he was and what he did. The saint knew that he could inspire the thief to change his outer habits and stop stealing. But it is hard to change someone who is lacking in core values. He knew that the inner virtues of the thief in regard to truthfulness were strong. He would not have to transform him in that way. He already had that quality of truthfulness within him. Thus, as a saint, he could stop him from the habit of stealing. Once he had done so, the man could then lead a virtuous life. But it is hard to stop someone who is prone to be dishonest. It takes a longer time to change one's nature than to change one's habits.

People who are weak and fearful might be dishonest. They may not want anyone to see who they really are. Thus, they may put up a false front. They may hide behind that front. No one really knows who they really are.

Thus, if we want to detox ourselves from untruthfulness, we need to take a look at our inner nature. Truthfulness is a quality of our soul. When we are truthful, it is reflected by the way we live. We are truthful in our thoughts, words, and deeds. There is consistency in everything we think, do, and say. It shows we have the courage to stand up for what we are and who we are. We become fearless. If we are not afraid of who we are, then why should we be afraid of others? It takes courage to be truthful.

We can cultivate truthfulness by connecting to our inner self through meditation. The more time we spend within through meditation, the more we connect with truth. If we connect with the Light and Sound within, we become connected with a place of truth. Then, we lose fear of others. We can be bold and courageous to be who we really are. We no longer have to hide. We can present our true self to the world. When people see that we think, speak, and act in an integrated way, we earn their respect and trust. We then can walk without fear. We can live our lives in strength and dignity as we walk in truth.

We can deeply consider the virtue of truthfulness and how it affects our lives. We can be truthful to both the people around us and to our true self within. When we detox our mind from falsehood, lies, and hypocrisy, we become transformed. We can achieve our highest goals of life and attain peace.

Exercise: Reflect on times in your life when you may have been untruthful and whether it affected your peace of mind. Use strategies in this chapter and spend time in meditation to connect with your inner strength and think about how being truthful in those same situations might have made you more peaceful and reduced your stress.

CHAPTER 13:

The Sweetness of Humility

Ego is a toxin that infiltrates our mind and disturbs our state of calm. Egotism takes many forms. It can make us think we are better than everyone and everything. It also means that we think of ourselves first, before considering others.

Due to its subtlety we may not be aware that we are poisoned by our ego. Egotism may seem harmless, such as when we think we are more beautiful or handsomer than others. If we feel more intelligent or more knowledgeable than others, it may cause us to look down on those not as smart as we think we are. We may consider ourselves stronger, more fit, or more talented or skilled than others. Our finances may make us feel superior to those who have less. We can have ego of name, fame, power, or position. For example, we may believe we should have a higher or more powerful position than others. The list goes on and on.

What may begin as a thought can escalate into words and deeds that hurt others. Egotism colors our behavior. It makes us think, say, and do hurtful things. It is one thing to harbor thoughts within our own mind that we are better than others, but once they are let loose into words and deeds, we create more problems for ourselves and others.

Relationships are harmed when we act with egotism. Once we harm others, reactions come back to us sooner or later and cause us pain in return. When we cause others to feel bad, they may retaliate against us. A cycle begins. Soon, what began as an egotistic thought boomerangs back to us. This causes us to suffer the reactions others have in response to our behavior, sending our mind into turmoil. The cycle of negativity is further fanned by the flame of egotism mixed with anger. People who speak and act egotistically can make others feel inferior, hurt, resentful, or angry. Ego leads us to make decisions at home or on the job that can bring pain to others.

Sub-categories of ego include pride of wealth, pride of knowledge, and pride of power. Any one of these presents a barrier to inner peace. Our mind becomes absorbed in thinking too much about ourselves.

In the past few decades, emphasis has been placed on the importance of building our self-esteem, whereby we feel good about ourselves. However, there is a big difference between having high self-esteem and being egotistic. Self-esteem is considered healthy because we feel positive about ourselves and the gifts we have been given in life. We feel happy when we set out to accomplish a goal and successfully achieve it. A student who studies hard feels good when receiving a high grade. A doctor who successfully saves a patient's life feels happy to help someone. These positive feelings motivate us to continue to do well. However, being egotistical enters a domain where our feeling good about ourselves is coupled with putting down others and hurting them when we think of them as inferior to us. Egotism is a poison to eliminate. It pollutes our thinking and defiles the environment in which we live.

Ego must be eliminated as it stands in the way of our own happiness. Yet, controlling our ego is a difficult challenge. At every turn, we face opportunities to boost up ourselves. Several antidotes can help rid ourselves of the ego that blocks us from attaining lasting peace:

- Developing the sweetness of humility
- Eliminating criticism by finding good in others
- Showing gratitude to the Giver

In the rest of this chapter we will see how these antidotes help us detox our mind from the ego to gain inner peace.

Exercise: Did you ever suffer from the toxin of egotism? If so, in which way did you feel you were better than others? How has it taken away from your own peace of mind?

Developing the Sweetness of Humility

Sweet humility is an antidote to eliminating our ego. When not content with ourselves, we boost ourselves up to appear better than others. We create a false identity thinking we are great, and others are less than us.

Meditation can help us overcome egotism. By tapping inside, we recognize that the Light within us is the same within every other person. When we become aware that the same Light illumines all, we stop seeing ourselves as being better than another. For example, if a variety of lamps shine with light powered by the same electricity, can we say the light from one is better than that shining from another? They are all run by the same electrical power. Similarly, the Light that gives us life and consciousness is the same within each person. Even though we may have different outer shapes, sizes, and backgrounds, we are all powered by the same inner Light.

Humility means we recognize that all are important. As spokes on a wheel need to work together to move a cart forward, so do all people need to work in harmony and synchronicity to make life on this planet run smoothly. Each spoke is as necessary as the others.

In this connection, there is a story of a carpenter. He was called to different homes and businesses in his village to make repairs. One night, when he left his toolbox in his shed, the tools held a meeting and talked to each other.

The hammer was the chairperson of the meeting. He hammered himself on the worktable to call the meeting to order.

After a few minutes, two of the tools protested and asked him to step down from being the chairperson and leave.

"Why should I leave?" he asked.

"You are way too noisy," the other tools told him.

The hammer said, "If I am too noisy and must leave, then the screw must leave with me."

"Why? What did I do?" asked the screw.

The hammer said, "You have to keep turning the screw around and around many times for it to be useful."

The screw said, "If you're going to send me away, then you must fire the plane."

The plane retorted, "Me! I'm so quiet. Why kick me out?"

The screw said, "All you do is shave off the top layer. All your work is on the surface. You have no depth. You're useless."

The plane said, "If you're going to fire me, then kick the ruler out, too."

The ruler yelled, "Why me?"

The plane explained, "You're always measuring everyone. Then, you think only you are right."

The ruler said, "Well, if you have to get rid of someone, get rid of the sandpaper."

The sandpaper screeched, "Hey, what's wrong with me?"

The ruler said, "You're so rough on everyone. You always rub people the wrong way."

The tools kept fighting amongst themselves all night long. Each tool thought it was the most important and that everyone else was incompetent or creating problems.

When morning came, the carpenter came to the shed to pick up the tools. He needed to carry them to a job where he had to build a stage on which a saint would be giving spiritual talks.

The carpenter used each of the tools to build the stage. He used the hammer, the screw, the plane, the ruler, and the sandpaper to build it. The tools all kept quiet in the presence of the carpenter as he worked using them.

At the end of the day, the stage was complete.

The carpenter surveyed the completed work and looked lovingly at the tools.

He told them, "Good work. You have all worked together to produce a stage where spiritual messages can be conveyed to audiences. All of us are working together and are equally important in the service of God."

The message of this story is that no matter what our flaws and faults, we are equally important. Everyone is different. People think, act, and work differently. Once we recognize the need to work together, we rise above our differences. When many hands are needed for any task, it is important to accept each other's differences for the job to be successful.

The story underscores the value of rising above our ego by developing humility. Each tool felt it was better than the other tools. This describes the egotism from which humans suffer. It is common to feel we are the only ones who have the right answers. We may think we are smarter and more powerful than everyone else. When working on a project we feel we know more than others.

When people work together on a project and each thinks he or she is right while others are wrong it is hard to complete the task. As with the tools in the story, time is wasted arguing over the points each wants to make. Thus, we delay the work. Sometimes it comes to a standstill because people cannot agree on how to complete it.

When ego causes people to fight verbally, it can turn into violence. Instead of discussing the topic at hand calmly, people degenerate into name-calling, backbiting, criticizing, or saying and doing harmful things to each other. The level of violence of thought, word, and deed can escalate beyond the original disagreement on a project. Harboring negative thoughts about others can lead to gossip or slander. Cliques form whereby one group sides with one person, and the other group sides with another. This is how communities divide into factions. Countries may even go to war. Long-standing feuds between families, communities, and nations develop, with some lasting hundreds and thousands of years. All this stems from the toxin of ego.

No one wants to work with others on a project and go home upset. They want to experience harmony. If we are instead mentally wrapped up in our ego, we close off the inner happiness trying to flow to us. We block the nectar of spiritual love when we do not work together in a spirit of humility.

The story of the carpenter and his tools concludes with all the tools despite their differences, working together to build a stage upon which positive messages can reach people. We are all cogs in a wheel rolling towards a bright future. We can equally play a part to make the world a better place. Through humility, peace can reach every human heart. We cannot let that noble goal be sidetracked by projects not getting done because people are focused on their ego, selfishness, or negative thoughts. By working in humility, we can enjoy the fruits of peace and love. We can then spread these to others to benefit us and the world.

Through meditation on the inner Light and Sound, we realize that the life-giving force within us is a gift we each have been given. Our life and talents are blessings. We may develop our talents through hard and focused work, but our innate nature was not of our doing. This attitude of recognizing that what we receive is a boon brings with it humility. While having self-esteem, we can recognize that others also are gifted and talented.

When we realize the good in others, we appreciate and respect them. We will not set ourselves above anyone, putting them down as inferior. While developing and excelling in our talents, humility means we do not get puffed up or make others feel bad. If we are born with certain traits through genetics or developing them by nurture, humility means not feeling egotistic and setting ourselves above others. We can appreciate what we have been given and make the best use of it.

By meditating, we wash away the notion that we are better than everyone, and instead we become grateful. This results in kindness to others. Our whole outer life becomes touched by gentleness.

Finding Good in Others

Some people promote themselves as knowing more than everyone else. They feel they know more than their bosses, professors, or trainers. This results in the mental toxin of criticizing others. Thoughts carry vibrations that ripple out far past the limitations of our physical skull. Even within the brain, vibration of thought does not travel in a direct line from one neuron to another. It skips over a gap between neurons, called a synapse. That space shows that thought is transmitted across non-physical space. If it travels this way in the brain, then think how those thoughts can also transcend the physical barriers of our skull. Science is starting to prove what saints through the ages have said about thoughts having an effect that can travel towards its target. Thus, when we think about someone, those thoughts travel and can affect the mind of the receiver. We know that the transmission of broadcasts in one part of the world can be viewed by people around the globe. Radio waves and light waves travel, crossing the boundaries of physical matter between the broadcast and the receiver. In the same way, thoughts have a far-reaching effect not constrained by the skull.

It is essential that we learn to train and tame the power of our thoughts. We are the sender. We can choose what thoughts we want to emit to the world. We are also the recipients of our thoughts. They not only go out to others, but they boomerang back to us. Like a pebble in the water radiates out in ripples, those ripples return to the stone's entry point in water. Nothing lives in a vacuum. The thoughts we emit have an effect on us, too. If we choose to send out arrows of angry thoughts, the effect of that anger ultimately returns to the archer who sent them—ourselves. If we choose to send out loving thoughts, we will be the beneficiary. It is up to us to choose whether we want an agitated or peaceful mind.

One common habit of our ego is to emit critical thoughts of others. We feel only we can do things right or have the correct answers and others are wrong or not as good. We find fault with everyone. This puts our mind in a tailspin. Instead of focusing on our own work we are busy complaining about the job that others are doing.

There is a difference between constructive criticism given in a spirit of goodwill to help others or to get a job done in a better way and criticism meant to put others down, make others feel bad, and not lead to any positive outcome. It becomes a toxin that keeps our mind engaged with negativity. Thus, we work ourselves into a stressful state.

Meditation can help us overcome negative criticism. When calm and filled with inner love and peace, we are gentle. We share our views to make a situation better in a loving way that does not make others feel bad or create rifts in a relationship. Giving positive suggestions encourages people to listen. They trust that we are not out to hurt them. More inclined to listen to us, they take our suggestions. Meditation enables us to speak calmly when we offer constructive criticism.

Think of a parent and child. Even though the child may resist the parent telling him or her how to behave or what to do for his or her own benefit, the child knows at heart the parent has love for him or her. He or she may rebel, but in the end knows the parent has his or her best interest at heart. Similarly, meditation makes us calm so that others know we have their best interest at heart and that the advice we are offering is meant to improve a situation or help others do better.

If everyone meditated, there would be more harmony at home, at work, or in the community. People would learn how to offer constructive criticism in a calm way to improve lives and make the world more peaceful.

In this connection, there is a humorous story about a father who took his young son to town to run some errands. While driving, when another driver cut their car off in their lane, the father yelled out the window, "You idiot."

CHAPTER 13: THE SWEETNESS OF HUMILITY

A little further down the road, the car in front of him stopped short for no reason, causing the father to yell, "Idiot!"

Another few miles further, the car in front of him stopped for a yellow light, instead of passing it, so the father again yelled, "You idiot."

During their journey together, the father called another five drivers "idiot."

When they reached home, the boy had lunch, and the mother had to take him to town for some other appointments. The drive was quiet and calm. The mother drove peacefully to the appointment and never said a word about any other driver.

When they reached the appointment, the boy turned to his mother and asked, "Mom, where did all the idiots go?"

The mom asked, "What do you mean?"

The boy said, "Half the drivers on the road this morning when I drove with my dad were idiots, but there were none this afternoon. Do idiots only drive in the morning? Where did they all go?"

This story illustrates the difference between living in a continual state of agitation and anger as opposed to living in a peaceful state of mind. The boy was the same in both circumstances. The car was the same. The roads were the same. What made the experience for the boy different from the morning until the afternoon? The significant difference was the state of mind of the driver. The father was in a continuous state of agitation. Thus, every perceived mistake he saw other drivers make on the road enflamed him. Normal activities one encounters on the road such as being cut off, seeing other drivers take risks, or getting the better of us happen all the time. If we choose to focus on that, our mind will be upset. On the other hand, the mother stayed centered in a peaceful state. She saw the drivers doing the same things on the road but ignored them and thus never encountered those whom her husband labelled as "idiots." That is the reason that the boy asked where all the idiots had gone.

All day long we encounter people. In our household when we wake up in the morning, on the way to work, at our jobs, or while shopping we meet people. Traffic annoys us. We are agitated by what is happening in the world that we learn through the Internet, social media, newspapers, radio, or TV. We are bombarded by news of others near and far. How we react to all such stimulation is a choice we can make.

If we choose to be critical, we cause our own mental agitation. We will be distracted by other people's thoughts. This not only upsets us at the intellectual and emotional level, but it affects our body.

On the other hand, if we choose to ignore the behaviors of others it won't affect our state of mind. We can observe and note what others do. We can either take action to rectify the problem or ignore it. We can choose to have peaceful thoughts and remain in a state of calm.

Those who are sports fans know how passionate we can be about our team winning a championship. When watching a game, we may become worked up. We may even yell at the TV when we see a bad play. The agitation of seeing our team lose not only lasts for a moment but there are fans who still cannot get over a loss for a long time. They are distraught. They chose to be upset.

However, if we were to watch a game with two teams we don't really care about, we may watch it but not get sick over what is happening. We do not let it affect our thoughts. We do not become emotionally and mentally critical and upset over the performance of either team. We avoid being so wrapped up in the results of watching the teams because our passion for either one is not invested. This is an illustration of how we can live in the world. We can keep a distance between what is happening and our thoughts.

Like the mother in the story who saw the same bad drivers on the road that her husband saw but chose to stay peaceful, we can, too. Whenever agitated by people with whom we interact, we can take a deep breath, focus within, and let the reaction pass. We can check our thoughts and nip them in the bud before we become agitated. There are many opportunities to experiment with this at home, at work, or at any place where we interact with others. With practice, we can tame our brain to keep agitated thoughts in check. Instead, we can cultivate peaceful thoughts.

Meditation helps us to choose calming thoughts. Each time we meditate, we are opting for peace. The time spent in meditation is one in which we still our thoughts and bask in a calm place within. The more we meditate, the more we carry that peace into the rest of the day. It is beneficial to meditate first thing in the morning before we face our day's challenges. We then enter the arena of life with a balanced attitude and are better able to drive through town like the calm mother in the story.

Introspecting our trend of thoughts can uncover the source

of our agitation. We will notice how often our thoughts stem from ego when interacting with others making us critical of what others do. Ego arises when we think we are better than others and criticize them for making mistakes. In whatever area we find we are mentally or emotionally agitated, we can do an experiment by checking our thoughts and stopping them before they have a chance to affect us. We can go through the day with a calmer attitude.

When we choose to submit to our egotistic critical thoughts, we stop focusing on the beautiful gifts within. Agitated thoughts deter us from keeping our attention on the highest goal of life, reuniting our soul with the Source from where it comes. If we choose peace of mind, our meditations will improve because we do not have to work so hard to concentrate. Throughout the day, we can stay focused within instead of finding fault while performing our worldly responsibilities. We can achieve the ultimate peace within.

Showing Gratitude to the Giver

Why is ego detrimental to our spiritual progress? Our ego prevents is from recognizing who is the Giver and the Doer in our lives. Ego makes us think we are the Doers and that we brought about the gifts we have in our lives. Recognizing that we are not the Givers, but the receivers helps us develop humility. We are here because of the grace of God. All the gifts we receive from being given a human birth to having the special faculty by which we can know ourselves and know God are due to God's grace.

Humility is recognizing that we owe gratitude to God for everything we have received.

To grow spiritually requires developing the twin qualities of gratitude and humility. One of the shortcuts to humility is to develop gratitude to God. When grateful to the Creator, we realize that whatever we receive in life is through God. If we develop gratitude, we will naturally develop humility and eliminate the ego.

Ego means we think we are the doers, while humility recognizes that God is the Doer. As long as we think we are the doers, we are focusing on the aspect of ourselves that is temporary and left behind when this life ends. The ego as a part of this physical world is only temporary. Humility connects us with the permanent part of ourselves, the soul, which is eternal.

Through the grace of God, we have been given a human form. We could have been born in any of the millions of species of life but have been fortunate to receive a human body. Besides a human body, God has graced us with many other gifts. Some of us may be rich. Others may be successful. Some may be CEO's of an organization, a king, a powerful businessperson, or the owner of a large factory. We may have become rich, famous, or powerful. If we look at people who have been materially successful, many think they have achieved that status on their own merits.

One of the banes of modern life is that people think they have achieved great material achievements on their own. They do not think that whatever they have is a gift of God. They forget that it is God who made them what they had become.

Similarly, we have forgotten that whatever we have become is due to God.

It is the trick of the ego that makes us think that whatever we have gained is due to something we are or have. We have forgotten that God has granted us certain gifts to enable us to achieve. We could be weak and helpless, but God has made us strong and powerful. Instead of being egotistic, we should use our gifts to do good and be grateful to God. We have the choice to do good with what we have or be egotistical and use our power over others.

We can lead a life of positive virtues. This also means putting in time for meditation. Along with this, we need to be humble. We should not be tricked by the ego into thinking that whatever we have achieved is due to us. We should recognize that God has given us all our gifts. Through gratitude, we can overcome our ego.

Ego is one of the vices to eliminate as we try to grow spiritually. Humility is the antidote for ego. With humility, we recognize that only God is perfect and that all of us are subject to failings and errors. We recognize that there are times we are right and times we are wrong.

There is nothing wrong with making a mistake, as it gives us a chance to learn and grow. When we make a mistake, we can rectify it and improve ourselves. Being able to admit our mistakes is a sign of humility. It makes life more peaceful and helps people get along when everyone recognizes we are all subject to failings and errors.

As we introspect, we should watch for incidents in which we dug in our heels convinced we were right even when others questioned us. We should then reflect on all the times that it turned out we were wrong but did not admit it, hid the fact even though it hurt someone else, or admitted it with reluctance. This failing needs to be weeded out for us to move forward in the area of humility. Next time confronted with our ego we can try to practice humility in our life.

Exercise: Reflect on aspects of your life in which you feel you were filled with ego. Notice how it affected your relationships with others. Attempt to curb your ego with detox methods from this chapter such as being humble, grateful for any gifts received in life, or finding good in others.

CHAPTER 14:

Love for All

When anger escalates to the point where it becomes unbearable, people often turn that anger on either themselves or others. We do not like the way we think, speak, or act when we are angry, so we chastise ourselves for allowing things to reach that point. Conversely, we blame others for making us angry. This can lead to hatred. We can't bear to admit we allowed ourselves to be angry. We don't like what we see when we look in the mirror and find an angry-looking person staring back at us. Rather than face the fact that we allowed ourselves to become angry, we lash out at others as "causing" it. We then turn our animosity towards them.

Toxin of Hatred

The toxin of hatred infests our mind to the point that we start thinking, saying, and acting in ways that are harmful to others and ourselves. The daily news depicts the results of a world aflame with hatred. Crimes against other people, discrimination against those who look or act different from us, and even wars are the result of hatred escalating to the point of violence towards others.

Hatred can infect even our daily home life or workplaces. It leads people to mistreat or ignore each other. It can even cause people to stoop to ruining other people's lives to get even with them over petty trivialities.

When the toxin of hatred infests our mind, it permeates our every thought and is reflected in our words. At times it makes us take actions that can destroy others and ourselves. Look how far away we become from peace and contentment when we allow the toxin of hatred to spread through our mind.

Exercise: Reflect on a time you may have felt hatred towards another. How did feeling hatred affect your mind?

Intolerance

Another toxin associated with hatred that plagues our mind is intolerance. There are several ways this poison takes away the peace we desire by leading to hatred. One way is that we become intolerant of other people's mistakes and develop hate for them. Another way is that we are intolerant of people because they are different from us, so we let it lead to hatred.

Intolerance of other people's errors can arise from our

ego when we think we are perfect and they are not. We set ourselves above others. Our ego comes into play when we think we're higher than everyone else. We may believe we're more intelligent or more clever than others. Assessing talent, we may believe we are better at a craft or art, while others lack skill. Engaging in intolerant thoughts means we're busy looking at what others are doing instead of what we're doing. Think of how more productive we'd be if we improved ourselves instead of others. Rather than being intolerant of other people's flaws, why not analyze ourselves and focus on how we can become better. However, when intolerance born out of ego escalates and morphs into hatred, it becomes even more dangerous. It is important to differentiate whether our intolerance for other's mistakes remains at the level of ego, or it flares up into hatred for others.

Another type of intolerance that can lead to hatred deals with our reaction to those who are different from us. We may have intolerance for other people's cultures or backgrounds. We may feel we are superior due to our culture, nationality, or background into which we were born. Another form of intolerance is not showing acceptance of people who speak a different language. Differences in social status or level of education may make us intolerant of others. Some look down on those with less wealth than we have. Such types of intolerance stem from feelings that our background is better than all others. The result of such thinking is that we may discriminate against others and treat them poorly.

All types of intolerance that arise from hatred percolate in our mind and interfere with our peaceful state. Every time we meet someone or hear about those who make mistakes or are different from us, intolerance causes us to be troubled by hateful thoughts we have against them. Thus, our tranquility is disturbed.

Exercise: Think back on times in your life when you may have felt intolerance and hatred to a person or a group. Reflect on the effect those thoughts had on your maintaining a calm state of being.

Prejudice and Bigotry

Two other toxins related to hatred are prejudice and bigotry, which are extremely dangerous. Prejudice and bigotry mean we feel one particular group of people is not as good as we are. We may be prejudiced against people of other countries, cultures, or backgrounds. We may have a bias against those who look different than us, based on the color of their skin, hair, or eyes, or any other physical features. We identify ourselves with a particular group and feel those in our group are better than those who are part of other groups.

Prejudice and bigotry are extremely toxic to our mind because they not only live within our thoughts; they can spill out into our words. We may say things that are not true and that are hurtful to others based on their differences. We may incite others to discriminate as we do.

Prejudice and bigotry can also manifest as actions. History is filled with accounts of the deeds committed by those who hurt others based on their prejudices. Bigotry has led to conflict, violence, and wars.

Once the toxins of prejudice and bigotry enter our mind,

we can become agitated whenever we meet or hear of people from groups different from the one with which we identify. In this way, we lose our mental peace.

Exercise: **List situations when you experienced prejudice and bigotry in your life. Think back on how those thoughts may have escalated into hurtful words or actions. Reflect on how those thoughts, words, or actions kept your mind from feeling peaceful.**

How Love Conquers Hate

In our life, we may meet others who for some reason do not like us or try to hurt us. Whether in our family, at work, or in our community, we may come across someone who criticizes us, slanders us, gossips about us, or tries to ruin our reputation. Intent upon bringing us down, they do not stop until they feel satisfied that they have damaged us. We wonder how to deal with such negative people. We feel that if we are nonviolent, we cannot retaliate or fight with that person. We try to hold our tongue so that no angry word escapes our lips. Yet, still, the person makes our life miserable and we do not know what to do about it.

We feel helplessness in the face of someone who is out to hurt us. This frustration and helplessness can turn to hate. We wonder what to do to either stop that person or protect ourselves from being hurt.

When hatred towards others fogs our thinking, people end up doing harm to others in thought, word, or deed. Like a pebble thrown into a pond causes ripples, the effect of hatred is far-reaching and wreaks havoc on society and the world. The hatred may be directed to others because they do not agree with us, or because they do not look, dress, or act like us. In the end, the toxins we spew out to hurt others only boomerangs to poison ourselves.

Meditation can be a preventative for hatred. Focusing within takes our mind off feeling hatred. It has a calming effect on our body and mind.

In this connection, there is an instructive true story from the life of United States President Abraham Lincoln. He is best known for ending slavery in the United States. His example has inspired many people. This incident in his life provides insight for us when we are faced with someone who is trying to hurt us and make our life difficult.

When Lincoln was on the campaign trail to run for president of the United States, there was a man named Edwin Stanton who did everything possible to make life difficult for him. He hated Lincoln. He would use every opportunity to mar Lincoln's image in the eyes of the public. Although Lincoln did not want to have any enemies, this man had set himself up as Lincoln's foe.

Stanton would say cruel things about Lincoln and make fun of his physical appearance. He used every opportunity to embarrass the presidential candidate publicly. Although Stanton persisted in his smear campaign, Lincoln won the election and became president.

One of the president's tasks was to appoint a cabinet of people who worked closely with him to implement his programs. There were important jobs such as the Secretary of State. As Lincoln began filling each position, he still had not appointed anyone as Secretary of War. The other members of his cabinet were shocked when Lincoln named Stanton for that position.

His cabinet members said, "How can you make him part of your cabinet? He did nothing but criticize and attack you during your campaign for presidency. You know what terrible things he said about you and how he smeared your image. How can you make him Secretary of War?"

One by one, each cabinet member strongly made the case that it was a mistake to put Stanton in his cabinet, saying, "He is your enemy. He will try to sabotage your programs to bring you down. You should consider all the bad things he did and said against you before making this decision."

Abraham Lincoln listened to the protests, but replied, "I am fully aware of Stanton and what he has said about me. Yet, after surveying all the possible people to fill this position, I find that Stanton is the best person in this country for that job."

Imagine the surprise when Stanton was informed that the president wanted him in his cabinet to serve in the important role of Secretary of War. Stanton took the position and worked hard to serve in that role to the best he could.

Lincoln was putting into practice one of his principles in life. He could have reverted to hatred. But instead he lived up to his own principle that if we want to get rid of our enemies, we should make them our friends. By being bold enough to ignore his own pride, Lincoln selected Stanton. The result was Stanton was so moved by the large-heartedness of the man whom he had tried to destroy that Stanton was transformed and became an able member of Lincoln's staff.

Years later, when Lincoln was assassinated, people who knew him spoke in his memory. Stanton, too, had words of eulogy for the president, which became some of the most well-remembered statements made about Lincoln. The man who was once Lincoln's enemy called him one of the greatest men who had ever lived, adding that he now belongs to the ages.

This inspiring example shows the power of love to wash away hate. Through his love for others, Lincoln could rise above the pettiness of hatred. He not only had the power of forgiveness, but he was gracious and could offer an olive branch to one who sought to bring him harm. He eliminated Stanton as an enemy by being gracious and making him a friend, one who would work closely with him as he carried out his monumental task as president.

If we look at the people in our lives who are giving us grief, we may find that our hopes to change them may not work. Our words to ask them to stop saying terrible things about us may fall on deaf ears. Asking others to intervene to stop these people from harming us also may not work. However, we still have one more tool at our disposal. If we put into action what Lincoln had done and make these enemies into friends, we could put a stop to their attacks.

How can we develop graciousness and make foes into friends? Lincoln was aware of what Stanton was doing, but he offered Stanton a job in his cabinet. Can we think of ways that we can approach those who are acting like our enemy and offer them something they may want? Can we find out what is important to them and help facilitate them getting their wishes fulfilled?

If we hear someone repeating gossip or criticism someone is spreading behind our backs, rather than retaliate, we can say something kind about the person, knowing that our words would make it back to his or her ears. What a surprise when they hear that the very person they are criticizing is responding not with hatred but with compassion.

The results of our loving ways may not happen in one day. They may not happen in one week, one month, or one year. However, our consistency in being kind and loving is bound to have an effect. Over time, they may realize that their attacks on us are not having any impact. The intensity of their hatred for us may lessen, and a day may come when they too become our friend.

The spiritual life is one of love. It is filled with compassion. If we remember the example of Lincoln and try to take each person giving us difficulty for no reason and make them our friend, we will find that we can transform them. The example set by Lincoln was so profound that the man who called himself Lincoln's enemy in later years gave him some of the highest praise. From enemies, we too can turn people into friends.

Each day we can evaluate how we respond to people. If others try to hurt or criticize us, we can make sure we do not respond with hatred. We can choose not to retaliate by hateful words or acts. We can avoid entering the fray by not saying bad things about that person. The hardest area to control though is our thoughts. Even if we don't say anything filled with hatred, we may be thinking hateful thoughts about the other person. A sign that we have advanced spiritually is being able to control our thoughts. If we can maintain a loving attitude in our thoughts towards that other person, then that will color our words, making them kind and loving. If our words are gentle and sweet, then our deeds will also be loving so that we do not do anything to hurt that person. When we live in this manner, we have put the example of the great saints and enlightened beings into our lives. We then become loving and even saintly as our actions will have the effect of transforming others.

How can we eliminate thoughts of hatred in our mind? Meditation can help us overcome hate. When we meditate, we are in touch with a calming, loving stream of Light and Sound. It has a soothing effect on us. It is like bathing in cool waters that wash away the grime from a hot, muggy day.

As we stay immersed in the Light and Sound within, we are uplifted. We reach a point in which inner Light sprouts forth. As we concentrate more, we are elevated to a state of consciousness in which we see that same Light shining in others. We see the Light radiating from other people, and even all forms of creation including animals, birds, reptiles, fish, and insects. This Light is not just a physical light made of inert waves that help our eyes see. This Light within is filled with bliss. When we connect with that inner loving Light, we experience that same love and Light radiating from others, and our joy abounds. We recognize that there is one Light of love glowing from all that lives. That love multiplies when we realize it shines in every person and living thing. Hatred melts away as we see the same love and Light that is in us is in all others. We then experience hatred turning to love through meditation on the inner Light and Sound.

By meditating and experiencing divine love within us, we

begin to act graciously to others. When we remember examples of those like Lincoln who turned hatred into love, we can incorporate that behavior into our own life. Over time, we can be loving and make enemies into friends, reduce the difficulties in our lives, and spread goodness wherever we go.

Overcoming Intolerance, Prejudice, and Bigotry through Meditation

Other toxins that stem from hatred are intolerance, prejudice, and bigotry that cause us to feel that certain groups of people are not as good as we are. Meditation can detox our mind from these. The intolerance, prejudice, and bigotry that people feel against those of other countries, cultures, or backgrounds because they look different can be replaced by acceptance. We no longer see one group as better than another.

Think about the attitude of doctors. They are trained to treat all people equally no matter whether their backgrounds are the same or different from theirs. Spending years studying the human body, they must look inside to study all the organs to learn how to treat disease or to operate on others. To them, a heart is a heart is a heart, no matter what the outer person looks like. Lungs are lungs. A brain is a brain. To doctors, all people have the same basic functionality. Similarly, when we recognize through meditation on the inner Light and Sound that the internal essence of all people is the soul, a radiant consciousness, we no longer focus on outer differences. We can eliminate intolerance, bigotry, and prejudice from our system when we see with our spiritual X-ray vision that the inner part of each human being is the same—a soul radiant with Light.

In this connection, there is a story from ancient India about a teen. He was a sweeper who lived in poverty. In those days, sweepers were considered untouchables. It was a time when there was a caste system in which people would not mix with the untouchables.

The teen was so poor he barely had enough money for clothes, shelter, and medicine. He had to sleep on the roadside. Yet, whenever people from a higher caste passed by, he had to get off the road so that his shadow would not defile others. If his shadow fell on people of a higher caste, they would scold and even beat him. His life was difficult. There was no hope for improvement. He was not even allowed to go to school to better himself.

One morning before dawn, he was doing his usual sweeping. He picked up the garbage from the street and carried it away. Carrying one basket of trash after another away he kept the road clean. While doing this work, he was full of sweat and grime.

One day, while working, he saw an entourage coming along the road. As the crowd neared, he saw it was the Buddha walking with a group of monks.

The teen was filled with a mixture of joy and panic. He was happy to have the sight of the Enlightened One. Yet, he was fearful because he was not to have his shadow fall on any of them.

He tried to hide, but there was a long wall along the road. He had no way to get out of the way of the Buddha. He put his broom against the wall and tried to squeeze himself as tightly as he could along the wall so as not to let his shadow fall on the

Buddha. As the Buddha neared, the teen folded his hands in respect to the Buddha, careful not to let them reach out too far to form a shadow on him.

Instead of walking passed him, Buddha approached closer to him. The teen tried to move further out of the way, but the wall was behind him, leaving him nowhere to go.

The teen was shocked when the Buddha came closer to him and spoke to him kindly.

The Buddha asked him, "Would you like to join us and become a monk?"

The teen's heart filled with joy.

He mustered up the courage to respond and said, "O great One. Never in my life has anyone ever spoke to me with such kindness and love. If you would accept such a filthy, low untouchable sweeper as me, I would gladly quit this work and become a monk."

The Buddha then accepted him as a disciple and let him join his group of monks. He taught him the meditation practice. Over time, the teen gained in spiritual enlightenment.

When the teen later asked Buddha why he accepted an untouchable like him, the Buddha replied, "Everyone, no matter what his or her color or background, cries the same color tears. Everyone sheds the same color blood when cut. When one is born, there is no high or low caste. It is our actions that make us high or low in ethical values. If we do good things, we are considered high in virtue. Each river is separate, but when each reaches the ocean, they all become one. Similarly, all are children of God and are one and the same, with no high or low. We should have love and kindness for all."

Saints and enlightened beings do not see any difference between people of different backgrounds. All are one and the same to them. That angle of vision is the key to turning intolerance, prejudice, and bigotry into universal love.

When we meditate, we see the same Light that is in us in all other people. We do not differentiate anyone because we see that Light shining in all. All of us are a part of God. All souls are our brothers and sisters in God. As one human family, we should be loving and kind to everyone. By doing so, we are living up to the highest ideals that makes someone truly human. By treating others kindly, we are showing respect not only to them but the Power who created all.

When dealing with others, whether family, co-workers, subordinates, and even strangers who are different from us whom we meet along the way, we should speak and act only with kindness and love. The good we do will not only heal the hearts of others but will come back to us. If we act kindly to everyone, even to those with different backgrounds, we have nothing to fear about our hurtful words coming back to us. We can sleep in peace knowing that we have spread loving kindness wherever we go and would never have to fear the retribution of unkindness and hatred.

Meditation expands our hearts to have love for all. We recognize all humanity as one family of God. As we walk through the highways of life, we begin to keep our eyes open. What does our life look like when we develop this love? We consider all people as part of our family. We no longer distinguish between people of one background or another or between those who are rich or poor. We stop distinguishing between those who are well educated and those who are not. This makes us aware of people who need help. We no longer only provide help for our loved ones but all we meet on the way. Love for all translates into selfless service to all. Our heart becomes large as to encompass all forms of life. Giving love means being kind and helpful to all. It means comforting others with our loving words. It can be as simple as a friendly, warm smile and greeting.

Meditation helps us overcome prejudice and bigotry so we become loving to all we meet. Our hearts are filled with joy when we love all. In this way we increase kindness and love in the world.

God is our role model. We are all created by God. All of us are God's children. Think of the world population of over seven billion people. There is enough room in the house of God, our planet Earth, for all of them. Each has the same faculties to survive. God does not just shine sunlight on some of them. All have access to sunlight. We are all created equally and have equal access to God's gifts.

More importantly, God has given each human being the faculty to know God. We all have access to the inner door, the seat of the soul, between and behind the two eyebrows. God is waiting to welcome each of us at that door. The welcome mat that God puts out for us is the threshold leading to the inner Light and Sound. God is calling us home to welcome us. It is only we who fail to notice the open door. When we connect with it, God then escorts us on the Light and Sound to reunite with God.

A child has no idea of how much love the parent has for him or her. No one can imagine the parents' love for a child until one becomes a parent himself or herself. In the same way, we cannot imagine how much love God has for each soul who is an offshoot of the Divine. We may feel as if we have been abandoned in this vast universe with no one to really love and care for us, but God loves each tremendously. God continues to love us no matter how we act. God created us and showered on us all the wondrous gifts of divine love, grace, bliss, and joy. The moment we seek God from the core of our heart and soul, God is ready to greet us with open arms and take us back.

Through meditation we can taste of God's love. We marvel at how God can love us even when we have ignored and forgotten God. The saints and enlightened ones know that we are coming from a life of habits that have kept us from God. We have habits such as being filled with hatred and bigotry. We can change these habits now so our soul can enjoy a mind detoxed of the poison of hate. When we replace hatred, intolerance, bigotry, and prejudice with love for all, we are in tune with the blissful peace that transforms our life into one of joy.

Exercise: One way to develop love for all is to think of people who are different due to background, culture, nationality, or other factors. Make a list of the ways that all those who you consider different are more alike to you than different. Think of ways to reach out in positive, loving ways to those who are different. Practice spreading love and kindness to whomever you meet.

CHAPTER 15:

Remove the "I" from Selfish to Become Selfless

Life in this world is like a land mine. It seems every move forward we are stepping on another poison that infiltrates our system. Desires may seem harmless, but they also can be toxic.

There is a difference between needs and wants or desires. For example, we have physical needs to help us survive. We cannot live without food, water, clothing, shelter, medicine, and transportation. We require jobs to earn money to pay for our needs. If we have families, we must support them. These constitute the basic necessities of life. However, beyond what we need to live, we may have wants and desires. These are things we generally do not need to survive but we want them to make us happy.

When we have what we need to live, we can be content. But

the toxin of desires makes us feel we cannot be satisfied without having certain things. It may take the shape of having more than what we need. It can also mean having better and better versions of what we need. Our whole materialistic society and the world of business focuses on advertising to make people want more than what they need to live. We may need a coat to keep us warm, but companies market coats that are either more expensive or have more embellishments than what we need. Each of us has our own likes and dislikes. Some of us may want a blue coat and others a black one. Some may want one with buttons and others with zippers. What is wrong with that? The toxic effect of desires arises when we either can't afford what we want and occupy our mind with many ways to satisfy our craving. Desires may also cause us to become so focused on getting what we want that we neglect other activities we should be doing instead.

We need to analyze the effect desires have on us. Is it taking over our mind to the point where we cannot think of anything else but obtaining the object of our desire? Is it making us act in a certain way that interferes with our normal life?

Think of a child who has a tantrum to get a new toy. When a child is disturbed he or she creates a racket to upset the peace of the household. Or a child is given a toy but after playing with it for a day tires of it and demands another and another from the parents. The unhappy child makes the parents distraught. Other children may demand that their parents spend more than they can afford for a special pair of running shoes because all the other children have that style. When a child wants its desires fulfilled, there is no peace in the home. It is the same with adults. We can think about what desires do to us. If it disturbs our peace of mind and takes over our attention, we know it is acting as a toxin.

A common toxin that disturbs our peace of mind is selfishness. The word "self" is related to thinking of our ego, or "I." Although in spiritual terms, the self can be equated with the soul or our inner essence, in terms of the mind it is related to thinking that we are number one and everyone else is secondary. It becomes toxic when in considering only our own needs we bring harm or pain to others.

Selfishness may start with a simple desire we want fulfilled. Although we use the word "desire" to equate with a need or want important for survival or attaining positive goals, it becomes a toxin when it has a negative impact on our life or that of others. If we desire something not good for us or harmful to those around us, then it becomes toxic. Our mind is focused on how to get more of what we desire. This leads to the poisons of selfishness, greed, attachment, possessiveness, obsession, envy, or jealousy.

The Toxin of Selfishness

Selfishness takes many forms. We can be selfish at a physical level. For example, physically, we think our comfort and needs come before all others. We want to make sure we take care that our hunger, thirst, and physical comforts take precedence over everyone else. This results in not wanting to share with others. It is an attitude of "me, me, me." We can see this in the case of children and teens, who have not yet developed a sense of sharing and selflessness. People usually grow out of this tendency when they become a parent themselves. Parenthood often reverses one's attitude as we learn to put our child first. For many, it is a new experience as we learn that for the child to survive, we need to think of his or her needs first.

Over time as we care for a family, whether a spouse, children, or aging parents, we generally rise out of selfishness to sacrifice our own needs to care for others first. Yet, the toxins of the mind are strong, and selfishness can creep in at any age. Thus, throughout our lives we still need to guard against thinking only of our own physical needs to also consider those of others at a physical level.

Selfishness can also attack us at a mental level. At school, we may want to grab all the attention in our class. We want the teacher to only help or notice us in the classroom. At our jobs, we can even be selfish about our work. While working on a team, we may want to do all the work ourselves, or we may let others do all the work while we take all the credit. If there are benefits or resources in the workplace, a selfish person wants to take everything for himself or herself without sharing.

When selfish, our mind is always on the lookout for opportunities to grab everything for ourselves. We are not in a state of calm, as our mind is on guard to take care of number one first.

Exercise: Look back on times you felt selfish, whether to meet your own physical or mental needs. In what ways did being selfish affect your ability to feel at peace?

Greed

The toxin of greed has several shades of meaning.

Amassing more than what we need and always thinking about how to get more can be another form of greed. Wanting more of something to help us or to make our life easier can be positive and lead us to take action to achieve it. However, greed arises when we attain what we want, but it is never enough. When wanting more occupies our mind to the point where we can't think of anything else, it can mutate into greed. Stereo-typical images depict greedy people never content with what they have and obsessing over getting more.

Desire becomes greed when we stop at nothing, crossing boundaries and rules to get what we want. Sometimes greed means taking from others instead of attaining something by ourselves. It may even escalate into hurting others to attain our desires.

When greed rears its ugly head, our mind becomes filled with thoughts that disturb our peace of mind. The contentment we once had that made us feel peaceful is replaced continually by thoughts of scheming to attain more.

Attachment

The corollary of desires is attachment. Once we attain what we desire, we can become attached to it. Attachment becomes toxic when we hold onto what we have in unhealthy ways. We cannot let go when we should. Our mind becomes filled with an object or person we consider as ours, and that is all we can think about.

We might be attached to an object, like a bicycle or motor-cycle. We then spend all our time taking care of it, shining and polishing it, adding embellishments, showing it off, and bragging about it to the point that we have no time left for anything else. We can have an item of clothing falling apart and even when it is time to discard it, we are so attached, we cannot let it go. We might then walk around wearing it in a torn condition. Money can be an attachment when we cannot use it to help our family or share with others. We can be attached to a person, feeling we own him or her, thus controlling his or her choices in life.

When we become so attached that we live in constant fear of losing something and cannot think of anything else that turns toxic. Loss is a normal part of life. However, when what we enjoy becomes a source of pain through fear of its loss or actual loss and we cannot function anymore, then attachment has become a toxin.

Possessiveness

Possessiveness is a form of greed in which we want to own what is not ours to own. We feel we have the right to something which is not ours. We may be possessive towards material belongings. In some cases, we do have a right to our belongings, but we do not want to give them up when it is better for us to do so. Some people want to collect and amass more than what they need of material objects. If this desire causes us to spend more on something we do not need at the expense of supporting our family or helping others, then we may have gone too far. Then our mind is occupied with thinking only of that which we want to possess with no space left over to help others.

Some try to possess other people. This results in exercising control over them when we have no right to do so. In some relationships, one partner may be trying to overly control another. People violate the boundaries of others in trying to possess them. This can happen in any relationship from family, to friends, to co-workers, or employees. It becomes toxic when we plan and scheme how to control another. When we feel possessive towards another, we are always watching what they say and do and intervening in their lives. We cause a disturbance in our own peace of mind and in the lives of others.

Exercise: Have you ever suffered from the toxins of greed, attachment, or possessiveness? If so, in what ways did it disturb your own state of contentment and calm?

Obsession

Desire, greed, and attachment can also lead to obsession where we cannot focus on anything else but what we crave. When the desire or attachment grows out of proportion and becomes destructive to our life or that of others it becomes an obsession.

While people can be attached to people in their lives, material objects, hobbies, or pastimes, it becomes toxic when it consumes our life to the point where we ignore other aspects of life that are important for our well-being or that of others.

Obsession is another poison that goes a step beyond attachment and desires. Obsession reaches levels where we are so attached or have such a desire for something that it becomes all we think about. We cannot get our mind off our desires or our attachment to whatever we attain. It starts occupying the rest of the activities we need to do, and we can't shake ourselves of it. We see people obsessed with sports to the point where they neglect their work and families. Some people are obsessed even with making money to the point where they work twenty hours a day to make more and more money than what they need, thereby neglecting their family and health. We see people obsessed with a hobby that they forget to eat or sleep to the detriment of their health. We can analyze how we spend our time and attention and if excessive towards one area, we may be suffering from the toxin of obsessiveness that has taken control of us.

Envy

Another shade of selfishness and desire is wanting something that another has to the point where we become envious. When we feel inferior about ourselves and wish we had what they have, this can lead to the toxin of envy.

Our peace of mind is disturbed by envy. In admiring others we might wish we had their gifts and talents. We might envy someone's beauty or physical form. Envy might stem from wishing we had the intelligence or skill someone else has. We might envy someone's wealth or possessions. A sports star may instill envy in those who wish they were as good. We could envy someone for their ability to write, paint, sing, act, or perform.

Sometimes envy can be positive as it drives us to improve ourselves to develop what others have attained or have become. However, the trouble arises when envy excessively occupies our thoughts. We may be so focused on the gifts of others that we no longer appreciate our own. We may have similar gifts, but when we think someone is better, we lose sight of reality. We no longer realize our own talents when we concentrate on looking at others. Thus, instead of engaging our mind to focus on the journey to reach our goal, we are busy watching and comparing ourselves to others. We waste time neglecting our own betterment by envying what others have.

Jealousy

Jealousy differs from envy in that we not only consider how others are better than us, but we also harbor negative, resentful feelings towards them. When envy is coupled with thinking harmful thoughts about the other person, this can lead to jealousy. Our mind is constantly jealous of what the other person has, and we even may take steps to try to take it from them. We can be jealous in relationships, about other people's academic or career success or their achievements in sports, arts, or hobbies. We can be jealous of people's physical characteristics or talents. Jealousy poisons our mind and deprives us of gratitude for the gifts we have.

When envious we usually hurt ourselves, but when jealous we may seek to take action against those who have what we want. If our mind thinks bad thoughts about those towards whom we are jealous, these thoughts can escalate into actions that harm others. We may spread untrue or harmful statements against them. Jealousy can lead to conflict between people. When this poison is released, it infects others. Then, others react to us and a cycle of violence ensues.

It is one thing to emulate others in a positive way, but it is another to hurt another person in words and deeds because we want either what they have or the gifts they have developed.

Exercise: Has envy or jealousy ever plagued you? If so, how did it affect your mental state of calm? What could you have better done to improve yourself rather than focusing on what others have or do?

The Toxic Treadmill of Selfishness

There is no rest when these toxins stemming from selfishness surge through our being. It is like running on a treadmill that goes at an ever-faster pace from which we cannot get off. The stress of these toxins increases, putting our mental health at risk. When we cannot get what we want or struggle to keep what we have we suffer from a lack of peace and joy. The end result of desires, attachment, possessiveness, obsessions, envy, and jealousy flood our mind. They keep us from spending time in areas more important for our physical, mental, and spiritual development. In this state of misery caught in the trap of selfishness, it is hard to be peaceful.

Exercise: Think of times in your life when you had toxic desires, attachment, possessiveness, obsessions, envy, or jealousy stemming from selfishness. Reflect on the amount of mental time you spent in these arenas. Were you peaceful during those times? What else could you have done with your mental energy to be peaceful if you were not poisoned by those toxins?

Replace Toxic Desires with Permanent Happiness

When we desire something material from this world, it cannot bring permanent happiness. Why? Everything in this physical world is made of matter. Thus, it is subject to decay or loss.

Material gains can break, decay, disintegrate, or be lost. Even a human being whom we love can leave us due to a disagreement, a move, or loss. Nothing in this physical world lasts forever. Thus, anything that we become attached to results in suffering when we lose it. When we seek our happiness through anything made of matter it has the flip side of suffering when we lose it. Thus, we can never find permanent happiness through anything in this material world.

What then can give us happiness? We can find lasting joy when we seek that which is permanent. Since matter is subject to decay, the only attainment we can seek that lasts is that which is not made of matter but is spiritual. We think we are merely the physical body, but we have within us a spiritual nature, which some refer to as the soul, the spirit, our true self, or our inner essence. Its qualities are consciousness, radiant Light, Celestial Music, spiritual love, bliss, peace, fearlessness, and immortality.

As long as we seek that which is temporary and made of matter, we undergo pain when we lose it. If instead we strive for what is permanent, made of spirit, we will attain a lasting happiness. Understanding the difference between temporary and permanent attainments can bring us peace and contentment.

We can rid ourselves of the toxins stemming from selfishness. While meditating we connect with the permanent joy within us. That brings its own inner joy that surpasses all the physical attainments of this world. Through meditation we can rid our mind of the toxins of selfishness and fill it with the permanent joy of selflessness.

Conquering the Toxins of Selfishness through Meditation

To overcome the toxins of selfishness and its resulting unhealthy desires, greed, attachment, possessiveness, obsession, envy, and jealousy, we can use meditation as a remedy. In meditation, we connect to an inner radiant musical current. The inner bliss is not like the brief happiness we experience when we obtain anything material; it is a permanent state of bliss which knows no end. Achieving our desires in this world is but a pale reflection of the joy we experience when immersed in the Light and Sound current. The inner experience puts us into ecstasy that surpasses any temporary happiness of this world.

We discover that in our search to fulfill our desires from the material world, we are basically looking for happiness. However, anything material is temporary and subject to loss. That which we feel makes us happy in this world can bring its opposite – unhappiness. When we meditate, we reach the source of happiness. It is a happiness that does not deteriorate. It is a joy we cannot lose. We merge with joy itself and are fulfilled.

Meditation washes away the toxins of worldly desire, greed, attachment, possessiveness, obsessions, envy, and jealousy. Once we recognize that striving to fulfill our desires for what is made of matter subject to decay that leads to loss, we can seek to attain the permanent happiness that meditation brings. The choice is ours as to whether to spend time looking for happiness in worldly material objects or tap into lasting happiness within.

Meditation can flush out the toxin of greed. We have to work hard to attain material gains, whether through honest means or taking from others what is not rightfully ours. Our mind becomes poisoned by the desire to get more of what we already have or what we seek from others. This prevents us from a state of contentment. However, in meditation, we receive a never-ending stream of happiness. There is no limit to the bliss available to us. We can enjoy as much of that ecstasy as we want. There is an infinite supply of happiness within that will never run out. There is not a limited store of joy that if we receive some, there won't be enough for others. There is an unlimited supply of peace for every soul in creation that lasts for all eternity. There is no question of greed as there is enough for all.

Being attached to something in this world that is temporary brings pain. Being attached to the inner treasures which are made of spirit brings permanent joy. The creative Power is eternal. It is all conscious, all love, all peace, and all joy. It cannot be destroyed and has no end. When we become attached through meditation with spiritual consciousness within us, we are then hooked up to eternal consciousness. We can never be separated from it as it is our own true nature. Meditation attaches us to that which is permanent, so we never have to fear or suffer its loss.

Obsession is the unhealthy focus on desires of this world where we cannot think about anything else. It is an ultimate poison as it drives our every thought, word, or deed. People can become obsessed with anything in this world, such as objects, addictions to intoxicating and hallucinogenic drugs, smoking, alcohol, unhealthy relationships, or other obsessions. We become fixated on something. Meditation can alleviate an obsession. When we taste joy within us, then the focus on our obsession drops away. By deriving a greater enjoyment from our connection to spiritual gifts, outer obsessions can melt away. Many people have cured their addictions to drugs, alcohol, and smoking by finding greater enjoyment in meditation. When they experienced the divine intoxication from meditation, the outer addictions fell away as they were not as satisfying.

Envy and jealousy poison our mind. Envy makes us want what others have. We can envy others without having negative feelings towards others. However, jealousy makes us feel ill will to those who have what we want. Both disturb our sense of contentment. We are not happy with our own situation. In envy, we are dissatisfied with ourselves. We do not feel we are as beautiful, talented, strong, wealthy, intelligent, powerful, or any other quality we feel others have. It leads to complaining about what we have and wishing we had more. In jealousy we not only want what others have, but it may be accompanied with a desire to hurt others for having that which we want, or we attempt to take away from them what is theirs. It can drive a person to do harm in thought, word, or deed. The poisons that are generated in our mind can consume us. Meditation helps us overcome envy and jealousy for we are embraced by godly love from within that washes away any sense of envy or jealousy we have of others. Anything of this world that we wish we had more of is replaced with a never-ending embrace of love, peace, and happiness.

When we meditate, we come in contact with a wellspring of joy and contentment. We discover there is nothing we can attain in the outer world that is as satisfying as the sublime bliss within.

Inside us is a spark of the Power that created all that is. Beauty, strength, intelligence, and other qualities connected to our physical body and mind can perish with age. Wealth and power are situational and subject to fluctuations in economics or positions in a company or institution. None of these last. Since they are temporary, we suffer when we lose them. Attaining what others have does not promise us lasting joy. Our material attainment does not guarantee our happiness.

Meditation puts us in touch with an inner source that provides a happiness not dependent upon us gaining outer gifts. It fills us with more joy than we can derive from outer beauty, power, or wealth. We no longer covet what others have because we realize we have spiritual riches.

When we meditate, we experience inner contentment. We pass each moment of life fulfilled as we have everything within and need nothing else.

Exercise: List sources of joy in your life that are not dependent on outer beauty, power, or wealth. Look for opportunities to spend time in those activities that bring happiness that do not depend on the outer material world.

CHAPTER 16:

The Joy of Selfless Service

When we look at the universe, we marvel at all forms of life that have been created. There are millions of species of life. The highest in all creation is the human being. But why was human life created? Why are we here?

In this connection, there is a story about a wealthy man. As he walked down a street, his eye caught a little homeless girl standing on the street corner. She wore tattered clothes and her hair was unkempt. Holding out a small cup, she begged passersby for food.

The man observed her but kept walking.

Reaching home, he sat down with his wife and children to a delicious dinner. His children were dressed well and owned many toys. His house had comfortable, beautiful furniture.

While enjoying an evening with them, his mind reflected on the poor little girl on the street.

As he thought about her, he suddenly became angry. How could such a small little girl be suffering? In his thoughts, he turned to God and said, "How could You let this happen? Why don't You do something to help the girl?"

To which God replied, "I did do something—I created you."

This one statement sums up one of the reasons we are here.

Animals live for their own survival. They eat to survive and reproduce. That is all they do. Human beings are the only form of creation that lives for others. When we realize this purpose we can overcome the toxin of turning a blind eye to the suffering of others.

It is said that God made humans to care for others. The story illuminates that whenever we question why God doesn't do something to help the poor, the needy, the suffering, God will tell us God did do something—God created us.

There was once a beautiful greeting card about Mother's Day, that said, "God could not be everywhere, so God created mothers." Another card said, "God could not be everywhere, so God created teachers." We can say the same about fathers, doctors, and nurses.

Each of us is an extension of God. One of our roles in life is to assist doing God's jobs. This includes living to help and give to others. We may give financial help. We may give physical help. We may give intellectual help. Saints and enlightened beings provide spiritual help. When we reach out to assist others, we are helping to do God's work.

However, there is one more person we need to help by doing God's work. We need to also help ourselves. Part of God's work is for each of us to realize God. While here to help others, we are also here to help ourselves find God in this lifetime. How can we do that? Saints show us how to truly help ourselves through meditation. By going within, we can find our true purpose. We realize we are soul, a part of God. Meditation can help us attain that realization of our true self and our Creator.

Once we realize the Light of God within us, we will then see the Light in all others. This will inspire us to help others. This quality of having love for all is a godly one. God wants all the children created as souls to love one another. While we may have outer differences of backgrounds or culture, we are all souls and all children of God. God does not enjoy seeing people fighting. God wants peace. God wants each soul created to live in harmony. God is pained when people kill each other. It is as painful as a parent watching his or her children hurt each other. Just as a parent wants to teach his or her children to get along, God also wants everyone in creation to get along.

Wisdom is learning to love one another. It is important to treat all people with love and tolerance. In every circumstance in life, we should exhibit the qualities of love and service. In this way, we will be spreading God's love wherever we go. God wants us to reach out to care for others. One of the characteristics of a true human being is to sacrifice for others. We should not only love our own kith and kin, but we should love all. Each soul is a part of God. Each is a creation of God. Each is a child of God. All souls were created out of love and affection.

A stage comes in the life of every soul when we start to

appreciate God's love. When souls want to reestablish their relationship with God that is the start of our spiritual awakening. God's love and affection for us is deeper than a parent has for a child. If we multiply a parent's love for a child many times over, we will still not get an inkling of God's love for each of us.

When a parent gives us love, we can get a small reflection of the love that God has for us. Unfortunately, we are souls enshrouded in a human body. The limitations of the five senses prevent us from communicating with God, who is spirit. The only way for us to see and speak to God is to identify with ourselves as soul. When we can shut down the outer senses and identify with our true nature, our true consciousness, then we can find God and know God's love.

Through meditation we can contact God's love. The soul is reminded of God's love for us. That love also pulls our soul within so we can find God in meditation. A saint's love has one purpose, which is to connect us with God's love within. It is a love that requires nothing in return.

When we attain God-realization we don't leave or negate our worldly responsibilities; rather, we continue our work in the world by loving and serving all creation. Then, we have fulfilled the two jobs God wants us to do: helping others and helping ourselves by finding God within. God is always there for us. If we turn to God in our times of need, God finds a way to help us.

If we become aware that humans were given the godly gift of having love and compassion for others, we would build a world where we would all join hands to help those in need. We would help those who are starving, homeless, struggling financially, and in mental or physical pain. If each of us helped others, we would have a world with less pain and sorrow. We also need to help ourselves by spending time in meditation to experience God within.

These are some of the purposes that God created us. Through meditation we help ourselves by realizing the Light of God within us and seeing the Light of God in all others. We can then consciously live our lives to give and be of service to others.

Healing Power of Selfless Service

Service has a benefit not measured in task completion. An unmeasurable benefit of selfless service is that it provides a healing power. Serving selflessly offers the power of healing to both the recipient and the giver.

In this connection, there is a true account that took place after one of the disastrous hurricanes that took place in the United States that resulted in such heavy flooding that people lost their homes or much of their belongings.

The hurricane force winds and floods swept many homes away leaving thousands homeless. For others, the rising waters reached as high as the second story of many homes and businesses. As a result, people in one-story structures lost all their belongings on the first floor. When the hurricane was over, the flooding continued washing away cars, boats, and belongings inside the home. All alike were affected, from the rich, to the middle-class, to the economically deprived. Hurricanes do not discriminate between the haves and have-nots and hurt them equally.

When the flood waters subsided and people were allowed

back from shelters to view their homes, it was devastating. For many, there was nothing left. As dry weather returned, people would look around their house to see if anything was salvageable. Wet photos of precious memories, torn and damaged clothing, a broken plate, or a piece of broken, wet, and moldy furniture were all that remained. Along with losing their belongings, many also lost their jobs as businesses were destroyed. Damaged storefronts forced owners to either file for bankruptcy or downsize as they could not afford to keep their workers on until they rebuilt.

As the holidays approached, people found they had no money to rebuild and replace. Their most cherished holiday activity of buying presents for their children, grandchildren, or loved ones was rendered impossible. They had no money to buy gifts, which pained their hearts the most.

One day, a grandmother received a knock on the door of whatever remained of her house. A kindly gentleman dressed as Santa Claus stood there showing sympathy for her situation. Through the open door the man could see inside a shell of a house, with carpeting and walls removed, broken furniture everywhere, and piles of destroyed materials. He reached into his pocket and pulled out something from an envelope.

"This is for you," he said. She saw he was handing her three crisp one hundred-dollar bills as a gift for her to use any way she wanted. Overwhelmed with tears, she thanked him. He was a stranger, but his kindness was overwhelming.

"I can use this to buy holiday presents for my grandchildren." She did not use it for herself but to give to others.

The man dressed as Santa proceeded to go from house to

house in this ruined town destroyed by the flood. One by one, he knocked on doors and handed out hundreds of dollars to people left destitute by the hurricane's floods.

When this charitable kind person, a stranger to all, had given out the money he was donating from his own pocket to people he met, he had one more task to do.

He called together the police department of that town.

When they gathered together, he told them, "Your example of heroism during these floods was an inspiration. Even though many of your own homes suffered damage and destruction, you went out on your duty going from home to home to save the lives of people trapped in the rising waters or in danger of being swept away. They put others as a priority before their own needs, even risking their lives to save others."

The man dressed as Santa then pulled out an envelope and proceeded to give money to each of the police officers and first responders as a gift of gratitude for their service to others. He gave each hundreds of dollars to use for themselves. The amount the man gave away was one hundred thousand dollars. The police were moved that someone would do that for them, enabling them to have money for the holidays however they wanted to use it for themselves.

The next day the townspeople noticed the police going through the town. They were going up to the people of the town who had lost their homes or had their residences destroyed, to homeless shelters, to people going to food pantries, and giving them each hundred-dollar bills. The people came to know that the police were so selfless that they had taken the money that Santa had given to them for themselves but instead were giving it to people in need. Tears of joy ran down the faces of people of all ages and backgrounds. Children, teens, parents, and people in their middle and senior years were filled with gratitude for their generosity.

What made the greatest impression on the townspeople was that many had considered the police as an enemy to be feared. They were under an impression that police were only there to arrest people or get them in trouble. For the first time, many realized police were human beings with a heart, just like they had. They recognized that the police also lost their homes in the floods and their families were struggling just as they were. The townspeople realized the police officers had left their own homes in devastation to risk their lives to save them. The unexpected reward that the generous stranger dressed as Santa gave them for themselves and families were being given to them with no thought of any return.

This generous gesture by the police brought a sense of unity between them and the community. They realized the police were there to help them. This brought healing to the community who now realized that the police in their community were also heroes who risked their own lives for the safety of others. No longer did people fear and reject them, but it healed and knit together the community. This holds up a model of how other communities can also start to heal.

This true anecdote shows the healing power of service. The hearts of the giver are soothed, healed, and filled with love. Giving also heals the hearts of the recipients, opening their eyes to the humanity of others.

The lesson we take from this incident is that selfless service is not only a job or task to be done; it is an act of healing, of opening hearts, and of radiating love. This cannot be measured by the number of hours one does, or the amount of a project one undertakes. It is an immeasurable gift that spreads love and healing wherever we go.

One of the greatest things a human being can do is to give of himself or herself to serve others. The truest form of selfless service is when we give without wanting anything in return. That is the spirit in which we should give. This means that we do not broadcast to others what we do to receive adulation, praise, power, name, or fame. Rather, we serve from our heart and soul in the spirit of helping others because it is the right thing to do as children of the all-giving Creator. This attitude has the power to heal.

Healing the World

When we lead a life of serving with a kind and patient attitude, we not only inspire those with whom we work, but others notice our kind qualities. People observe something special about us. They see we are calm and collected. They see us facing life's challenges with nonviolence, love, and humility. They watch how we give freely of ourselves selflessly. These traits will attract others to want to lead such a selfless life. This shows the power of being examples and modeling the positive values in our everyday lives. By not only talking about it but living a life of selflessness, we can inspire others to do the same.

How we perform selfless service can detox our mind. When we serve, we can choose to act virtuously or negatively. There are times when things do not go our way, such as when we have to wait. Are we angry and impatient, or do we remain calm? If we end up getting angry, then our service is no longer selfless. Others will wonder what benefit service has if we are still violent. When we are impatient, we are letting our ego get the better of us. If we are trying to spread God's love to others by serving but are impatient in the process, then we are not setting a good example. People will notice our anger more than the service we are doing. True service is performed when we remain calm even when a situation is not going our way.

We can detox our mind by watching how we act in various situations and make sure we develop patience. We can extend our service from people to animals, plants, and the planet.

Selfless service strengthens our spiritual development. Our words and actions arise from our thoughts. If we have thoughts in which we want to help others, then that will cause our words and actions to reflect that. If we are going to talk of the need for selfless service, we should practice it ourselves. Rather than telling everyone else or criticizing how they serve we have a greater effect by serving selflessly ourselves as an example.

When our selfless service is completed, we can then sit in meditation to enjoy the benefits. Even if we are engaged in service that requires long hours, when we are finished and sit in meditation we can taste the fruits of that service. If there is a deadline, we can also take short breaks in which we sit in meditation before resuming our service. When our duty is completed or our deadline is met we can meditate to experience the spiritual benefits. After doing selfless service, our attention will be more focused within and we will be more receptive. This can accelerate our progress to experience the inner manifestations of Light and Sound and reunite our soul with God.

There are many wonderful selfless service projects happening throughout the world. No matter how different our backgrounds are, we are all one family in God. This attitude of loving and accepting people who are different from us is fundamental to selfless service. We realize that service means more than just helping people who are like us but everyone different from us. As the stranger dressed as Santa helped people different from himself, and, in turn, the police in turn helped members of their community different from them, we too can learn to love all and serve all.

Through the healing power of selfless service, it helps the receivers as well as healing our own hearts and healing the world.

Carry the Load of Another

There are many ways to be of service. Some selfless service involves working alone. Another type is to pitch in to help others carry their loads.

In this connection, there is a story about a man who was an influential leader in his country. When travelling through town, although he was wealthy, he dressed simply so no one would recognize him.

During one of his walks he saw a poor worker carrying a heavy load on his back. It was so heavy that the man's back was painfully bent over to support the mass. He walked with slow steps so as not to drop the load or fall.

DETOX THE MIND

The wealthy leader feeling compassion for his situation said, "May I help you carry this heavy burden?"

The worker did not recognize the man as one of the leaders of his country, so he agreed to turn over his load. He put the load down.

The great leader picked it up and strapped it on his own back. He carried it all the way to the final destination.

When they reached the place where the load was to be delivered, the leader put down the load. He then reached into his pocket and took out some money to give to the worker and asked him to bless him. One would think it was the worker who would give the man a tip for carrying the load, but the leader gave the man money instead.

The worker thanked the man. The leader did not want any recognition or money for what he did. He just loved to serve quietly and selflessly.

This is what true selfless service is. We do something to help another without wanting any reward.

Carrying someone's load may be a physical task like helping to lift a box, move a piece of furniture, or carry groceries home for someone. It can also be an intellectual task where you help someone solve a mental problem or do work like helping someone with homework or helping to put letters into envelopes for a mailing.

The beauty of this story is that the man was a known leader, but he went into town incognito to do good without wanting any praise or reward for it. He did it out of the love of helping others. He did not want money for his work, but actually gave his own money to help the man.

166

CHAPTER 16: THE JOY OF SELFLESS SERVICE

Some types of service are done in an anonymous way. Others do not know who is doing what. We may be doing our service unseen by others so those who benefit from it do not know who has played a part in it. There are many jobs done behind the scenes and no one knows who is doing the work.

Selfless service can sometimes be known to others and sometimes it can be anonymous. Both types have value and are spiritually beneficial if done selflessly.

There are many opportunities for providing assistance to people in an anonymous manner. When there are hurricanes, earthquakes, floods, fires, or Tsunamis, we often send help in the form of food and medicine, and the recipients do not know the specific person from whom it came. When we work as a team on a project, those who benefit from it do not always know who did what part. They may know in general who is involved but our specific work is not known to people. They may know someone is volunteering, but they do not know the name of the person who did it. Our service is then being done anonymously. Sometimes we just want to do something nice for an individual and leave it for them without any note. We may cook something for someone who is ill and cannot cook for himself or herself. We may get flowers or bake cookies for someone. Sometimes we may just leave a little surprise for someone and enjoy the pleasure of knowing we made him or her happy.

Both types of service—those in which people see what we are doing and those in which no one sees—are equally good, as long as done selflessly. Our job is to keep our eyes open for opportunities to help others whenever we can, whether physically or financially. Although we should not seek physical or financial rewards for selfless service, we will discover that we will be blessed at a spiritual level by God and our spiritual progress will accelerate rapidly.

We should walk through life noticing other people. When we see others struggling with a load, we can offer our help. Maybe they take it, or maybe not, but at least we should offer. Meditation helps us connect with the inner Light within us. As we are more connected, we realize the same Light in us is in other people. As brothers and sisters, all part of one human family of God, we are moved to provide help to others.

We Never Lose When We Give and Serve Selflessly

One of the greatest things a human being can do is to serve others. Many fear giving because they worry they will have less. They do not realize there is a law of abundance at work in the universe. Whenever we give selflessly, we end up having more.

People tend to believe that when they give something away, they have less. Our thinking is limited to our observation of matter. We think if we have five apples and give away three, we only have two. That is a law of science and math by which this physical world operates. However, there is a higher spiritual law operating in creation that has its own set of rules. If we pay attention to situations that occur throughout our lives we discover there is more to these hidden laws. When our spiritual vision opens, we find that it is not necessarily that we have less when we give something away.

We never lose when we give and serve selflessly. Many times in life, we may have experienced an opportunity to give something away to someone in need, making a sacrifice, only to find that it was either returned to us or circumstances changed and we did not need to give it away. Yet, we were rewarded with the feeling of satisfaction of having sacrificed for others. We feel God's blessings showering down upon us.

If we are selfish, we often find ourselves filled with remorse and regret. We always feel sorry that we did not give. However, one never regrets or feels sorry for giving. We are richly rewarded not only in this world, but also in the world to come. There is no greater joy that can fill our heart than giving. All those who have ever given selflessly would have experienced that one never loses when one gives. One finds more blessings raining down unasked for, and their heart is filled with godly love.

How many times do we do acts of goodness when we want to impress others? Do we find that in our offices we speak humbly and kindly to our boss, but speak abusively to our co-workers or subordinates? How many of us give only when we are on display for others to see how generous we are, yet in the loneliness of a street we walk cold-heartedly past a beggar?

Let us give from our soul. Our mind gives for selfish reasons. It wants praise from others. It wants respect from others. It wants to make a grand show of how kind and loving it is, when, in reality, it is self-serving. Soul gives for the sake of giving. Soul gives out of a sincere desire to help others. It wants nothing in return. It does not even wish to be known for what it has done. When the soul gives, it is the God within us giving. Just as God does not want anything in return for all the wondrous gifts of creation bestowed on all forms of life, so does the soul give selflessly.

To be in tune with God, we can give from the soul, selflessly, lovingly, without any show and without any thought of return. We do so as we only want to serve and relieve the suffering of others. That giving from the soul has the power to heal others. We discover that when we give, we end up having more.

In this connection, there is the story of a family with a husband, wife, and three children. They were doing well financially, until the husband died. Because he had no savings, there was no money for the wife and children. They soon sunk into poverty. The woman did not have a job so there were no funds to feed herself and her children.

The only thing that kept her going was her faith in God.

As there was not enough food, her children asked her what will happen.

She told her children, "Don't worry. God will provide."

The woman went to a rental store and found a sewing machine. She thought she could earn money sewing clothing to sell. She was able to scrounge up enough money to pay for the first month's rent and buy some cloth and thread.

While the children slept, she stayed up late sewing clothes to sell. She used the money to pay for her children's food and for schoolbooks.

At the end of the month, it was time to pay the rent on the sewing machine. However, she had used up all the money on their food and living expenses. The man who collected rent for the machine sent her a warning that if she did not pay up within twenty-four hours, he would take back the sewing machine.

On the day that the rent money was due the children huddled with their mother.

The young ones cried, "What will happen now if he takes back the sewing machine? How will you be able to sew clothes to sell so we can have food to eat?"

Suddenly, there was a knock on the door. The children hid in fear of the man who was coming to take the sewing machine away.

The mother told them, "Do not hide in fear. There is nothing to be afraid of. God will provide."

The mother opened the door, thinking the man who rented her the equipment was coming. But instead, she saw a different man at the door. She had never seen him before. He was holding a baby.

The man was upset and said, "Please, can you help me? My wife has become sick and is in the hospital. We don't have anyone at home to take care of the baby. I have to work, but do not have a babysitter to watch the child. Since I just moved into the neighborhood, I didn't know who to ask for help. People gave your name and said you were a kind woman with children of your own and could care for the infant until my wife recovered."

The mother being generous and caring said, "Yes, I will take care of the baby."

Her own children tugged on her skirt to pull her into the other room. She went with them, and they said, "Mother, how could you care for this child when you barely have enough money to take care of us?"

The mother said, "Don't worry. God will provide."

The mother returned to the front door and told the man,

"Yes, I will watch your child while your wife is in the hospital." Tears came to his eyes and he thanked her profusely.

He handed her the infant. She hugged the baby giving him confidence the child was in loving hands.

While leaving, he left her an envelope. When he had gone, she opened the letter. Showing it to her children she smiled and said, "You see, God does provide."

In the envelope the man had left money and a note saying, "Here is money to take care of the child. I will pay you this same amount each week." When the woman counted the money, it was not only enough to pay for the rental of the sewing machine that she owed the man coming to collect but was enough to pay for the family's food.

She thanked God for truly providing for her and her family.

If we reflect on our lives, we may recall times when things seemed dark and dismal. We may have been faced with one problem after another. But as we recall those times, we may find that even while having our own difficulties, when we reached out to others God truly provided in the end and everything worked out fine.

The physical laws of this earth might lead us to believe that because the woman had barely enough to feed her own children and no time left to take away from her sewing to watch the baby that she should have refused to help the man. She neither had the money or time to give away. But she had faith in God and knew that God would provide if she made the choice to give selflessly. Thus, she chose to take care of the baby, not knowing the man was even going to pay her.

She was glad that even though she did not expect any

money, after she accepted to help him that he not only paid her for her time watching the baby but gave her more than enough. This enabled her to have the money in time to pay the rental fee for the sewing machine. It also provided a cushion to keep feeding her children and paying the house rent no matter how much she sold of the clothing she stitched. The woman ended up receiving much more than she would have ever asked or hoped for.

This example is one of many we may find if we open our eyes to the spiritual laws operating in the universe. For those who give selflessly, God provides.

Through introspecting each day we can note how many opportunities come our way to share with others without wanting anything in return. Just like the woman who gave selflessly even when she thought she could not from a physical standpoint do so, she gave anyway. We can see how through her giving, God provided to her. God not only gave her equal to what she shared but provided more in return. These are spiritual laws hidden from our physical eyes. When we live by spiritual laws, many blessings will shower on us. These experiences give us faith to make it through tough times.

Just as the children were fearful of their fate, their mother relied on her faith in God's goodness and spiritual laws to know everything would be all right. We can try out these principles in our own life. We can always be ready to give and help. We should not lose hope in troubled times but put our faith in God that all things will work out in the end. We do not lose when we give.

Through selfless acts coupled with meditation, we can experience these spiritual laws and see how God's goodness and abundance work in our lives.

Exercise: Reflect on times that you performed service selflessly and how it made you feel. Compare that experience with times where you were rewarded materially for your service. Did you notice a difference between serving without wanting a material reward with times you did receive back something unasked for, for your help? List ways you can add opportunities to your life where you selflessly serve others.

CHAPTER 17:

Meditation: Solution for Stress, Fear, Anxiety, Panic, and Worries

Stress, Fears, Anxieties, and Panic

Stress and fear are natural physiological responses that serve as a warning system for survival. They signal to our brain to take action to protect ourselves or our loved ones. Without them, we may be oblivious to threats to our life. They begin with a sense of danger and a corresponding increase in blood pressure to get us ready to run or fight. Our heart pounds. Our chest tightens. We are getting ready to react to save ourselves.

However, in today's world we often react to common triggers of life with the intensity of a life-threatening event. Someone cuts off our car and we go into road rage. A family member doesn't pick up something they dropped in the house and we lash out. Someone does not agree with us and we verbally attack their character. We do not get what we want and throw a tantrum. All these actions are preceded by a fight or flight response. Stress, fear, anxiety, and panic trigger the release of cortisol and adrenaline into our system that floods our body and mind. Logical and rational thinking becomes replaced with the fight or flight reactions. We become far removed from a state of calm and tranquility.

Consider how much of daily life is consumed with stress, fear, panic, and anxiety. Situations at our work or at home activate these toxins. Traveling to and from work triggers stress. Financial, health, family, and relationship problems set stress and anxiety into motion. When we do not find solutions for these we enter into states of panic and fear.

Besides our personal problems, a daily barrage of news from our community, our country, and the world adds to our fear and anxiety. Hearing about natural disasters, wars, epidemics, violence, economic instability, and poverty upsets us. When we do not see solutions offered for these it increases our stress and fear.

Living with fear, stress, anxiety, and panic stirs up dark whirlwinds of toxins that keep us from leading a life of peace and calm.

Exercise: What incites fear within you? What causes your stress in life? Reflect on times you felt anxiety or panic. Reflect on how far from being happy and peaceful such states of mind caused you. Consider how much joy you would have if you could eliminate these toxins from your mind.

Worry About the Past and the Future

Even if we are fortunate to manage the host of the toxins of fear and stress that bombard us, two more find their way into our system to prevent us from tranquility—worry about the past and future.

Worrying about the past involves regrets about what we cannot change. The past is over. We cannot alter what happened. Yet, the toxin of ruminating over what transpired keeps us from feeling peaceful. Like a video replay of a catastrophe, we relive the trauma over and over, stirring up reruns of toxins. Some become obsessed with past traumas and cannot focus on what is happening in the present moment. If the trauma was severe, people suffer from post-traumatic stress disorder (PTSD) and any similar trigger even if minor can produce the same intense fear and panic as one experienced during the initial pain. On a lesser scale, we can analyze how many times a day we rethink what already happened and undergo pain, regret, and worry. The current moment in which we should focus on the here and now in a peaceful way is usurped by memories of past regrets.

Alternatively, we may also suffer the toxin of worrying about the future. We imagine all the things that can go wrong and become anxious about what tomorrow will bring. Instead of facing situations as they arise, we project scenarios that might happen and become panicked. However, when time passes and we look back, much of what we feared could happen never took place. We wasted many moments in made-up scenarios instead of focusing on the reality of what was happening in the current moment. The toxins of worry about the future eat away at us and rob us of peace and happiness.

Exercise: List your worries about the past. Then, note the worries you have about the future. Consider how much time you spend in each and how they prevent you from experiencing the current moment. Think of the peace you wish you could feel in the current moment, and how that is being eaten up by worries of the past and future.

Overcoming Stress, Fears, Anxiety, Panic and Worries

Toxins that wreak havoc with our physical and mental health are stress, fear, anxiety, panic, and worry. These trigger the release of hormones that result in stress-related illnesses. We are pulled into a downward spiral which many cannot climb out from on their own. Unfortunately, some turn to drugs and alcohol to deal with these toxins thinking those are the solutions. However, chemical methods with their risky side-effects may compound the original problems.

Stress, fear, anxiety, panic, and worry arise when we face the unknown. We project what will happen to us in the future. We remember past events that brought us harm and worry about facing those again. We also may imagine all the things that can go wrong to hurt us. We mentally worry about potential fears that may or may not happen. Fear is important when facing a true threat to our survival, which triggers the fight or flight response to protect ourselves. However, fears, anxieties, and panic can be triggered by our imagination. When not faced with a real threat, if our mind imagines it is in danger, we release hormones that can have harmful side effects to our body and mind.

Meditation provides relief from stress. It can reduce fears caused by worrying about something that may or may not happen. Once our mind is calmed, we can better face our fears.

In this connection, there is a story of a boy brought up in a mansion. When his parents were going on a trip, they asked a relative to stay at home with him. Before they left, they told him not to go to the attic, but didn't give him a reason for forbidding him from going there. While their real reason was that there were many family treasures they did not want him to break, they did not explain to him. What happens when our parents tell us not to do something? The first thing we want to do is the opposite of what we were told. As soon as the boy's parents left, he wanted to go to the attic.

 Having never been to the attic before, the boy thought it would be fun to see what was there. He climbed up the stairs to the attic on the top floor. The steps creaked from age as the mansion was hundreds of years old. Reaching the top, he saw the attic door padlocked. He peeped inside a large keyhole to see what was in there.

Suddenly, he got the shock of his life. Peering through the keyhole, he saw a large monster staring back at him. He screamed and rushed downstairs as fast as he could.

On the main floor of the house he sat down, trembling with fear. He had lived in that house for many years with his parents and never saw this monster before. No one had ever warned him about it.

The boy thought to himself, "Maybe the monster is locked in the attic and cannot get out. Maybe that is why we have never seen it before. What happens if it gets out? If I'm here all alone he might kill me. What if it gets out when my parents come home and kills them?"

He did not want to tell his relatives or call his parents to tell them about this as they might think he was weak and helpless.

"I know what I will do," the boy thought to himself. "I will become big and strong and kill the monster myself. I will work out and build my muscles. By learning archery, I could shoot an arrow to protect my family from this monster."

The boy spent day and night exercising and using weights to build his muscles. He joined an archery class to master the bow and arrow to protect his family. His whole time was spent in preparing himself to battle the monster. He was determined to gain the strength he needed before his parents returned, as he did not want the monster to harm them.

Soon, the boy's whole attention was on slaying this monster. Unable to think about anything else, he stopped playing with his friends after school or doing the enjoyable things he had done before. He could not focus on anything but preparing to slay the monster in the attic.

The day before his parents were scheduled to return home, the boy decided he was strong enough to take on the monster. His muscles had grown strong and hard. Dressing up in the armor kept as a decoration in one of the rooms of the mansion, he readied his bow and arrow.

He selected a strong hammer to break the padlock. When he reached the top of the stairs, he quickly broke the padlock and swung open the door. Mustering all his courage, he quickly aimed his arrow and shot right into the heart of the monster.

Suddenly, bird feathers and cotton were flying everywhere.

He expected the monster to fall on the floor with the arrow through his heart, but instead found the monster was nothing but a life-style stuffed cotton doll! All this time he thought there was a monster in there, but it was nothing but a large, toy monster.

The boy realized that what he had feared and devoted his whole time in preparation to destroy was but a figment of his own mind. He had taken the monster to be real. The fear he lived with was only a result of his own mind playing a trick on him.

This is what happens to us. A large portion of what happens to us in life is taken to be a dreaded monster. Trivial things are blown up into large fears that cause us anxiety and panic. We spend our lives trying to slay the monster of our fears only to discover they are made of mere cotton. We spend much of our entire life's breaths battling illusionary threats.

How can we detox our minds from these fears and worries to live a life of peace?

Meditation is a solution for the toxins of stress and fear. How? Through meditation we connect with an inner strength that empowers us with fearlessness. We are put in touch with an inner spiritual power that gives us calm and equipoise.

A child who fears the darkness and imagines all kinds of monsters in the closet or under the bed shudders. However, when a parent comes to hold and comfort him or her, the child feels safe. Similarly, when we tap into our inner essence which is connected to the Power that created all, we experience security and comfort. We still take outer steps to protect ourselves against true threats, but we are touched with a sense of stability from a Power greater than us that helps fortify us against needless worries. The more time we spend in meditation on the inner Light and Sound, the more we contact the inner source of strength and fearlessness that washes away unfounded fears.

When we feel fear, anxiety, or panic, we can list what is causing it. We can then ask ourselves whether it is a real threat to us or are we just worried about something that may or may not happen. If it is real, we can make an action plan to protect ourselves. While taking action, we do not need to also let the toxin of worry continue to surge through us. By meditating, we can enter states of calm, so we can realistically evaluate the situation. If a threat arises, we have a plan.

However, if we analyze a situation and realize it is only an imagined threat, meditation can keep us calm. Meditating provides balance and stability so we can discriminate whether there is something to fear or just the unlikely possibility of something. We can then prepare ourselves for any eventuality but not let fear and anxiety poison us when there is nothing threatening us.

Overcoming Worry about the Past and the Future

Worrying about the past and future pulls our attention away from the current moment. When we are at a spa retreat, nature with all its glories abound. Our body is rejuvenated in a spa where warm waters bathe us. All is well. The current moment is filled with peace. But suddenly our mind might take us back to pains from our past. It may also pull our attention into fears about the future. The peacefulness is stolen from us by these past and future worries. We cannot change the past and cannot predict the future. We are worrying about something we cannot change or something that may or may not happen.

Meditation provides relief from worrying about the past and the future. When we become absorbed into the inner Light and Sound we are transported to bliss. The current moment is spent living in eternity. We tap into a state of all-consciousness, bliss, and love from contact with the inner Light and Sound. The pains and sorrows of the world dissipate. The toxins of past worries and future fears are washed away. We are in an eternal moment of perpetual bliss.

An example of being worry-free is when we are in a state of love. Time and space are forgotten. We do not think about the past and future. Instead, we live in the now and its joy. Being absorbed into the stream of Light and Sound awakens inner bliss. Past worries and future anxieties dissipate.

Through meditation, past unhappiness is replaced with happiness, past anger by nonviolence, past anxiety by peacefulness, and past hatred by love. No matter what problems one faces in life we are soothed by the upliftment and joy of meditation.

Putting Our Worries in God's Hands

Life is filled with challenges. Daily, if not hourly, something goes wrong that causes us worry. We may have a financial crisis, health difficulty, or relationship problem. Often, we have more than one challenge at a time knocking at our door.

At the same time, we are told that worry is bad for our

health. Doctors advise us that worries can cause stress-related illnesses. How can we deal with all our problems without the risk of stress causing us to fall ill?

In this connection, there is a story of a man who was walking by the shores of the Dead Sea. Preoccupied in thought he was not watching where he was going. His foot slipped on a rock and he fell into a deep part of the sea.

Not knowing how to swim, he panicked. He thrashed his arms and kicked his legs but unable to swim he was unable to move out of the deep waters. He kept moving his arms, but it only made him more tired. When out of breath and his limbs could no longer thrash about, he realized he was about to die.

He thought of all the things he still planned to do with his life and was saddened he would never be able to achieve them. Exhausted, he mentally prepared to die. With no energy left, he stopped thrashing around, so finally he gave up, and just lay there in the water, preparing to drown.

He lay there ten seconds, twenty seconds, thirty seconds, a minute. He was shocked to be still alive. The man realized he was not sinking but peacefully floating on top of the water. His body and muscles were totally relaxed. Calmly, he floated.

Suddenly, he realized where he had fallen. He had forgotten he was in the Dead Sea. This body of water contains so much salt and minerals that one could easily float in it. If he had realized this, he could have avoided his worries and fears about drowning and put his trust into the waters that would keep him afloat.

This story provides a lesson on how to overcome our worries. One key is to put our worries into God's hands. Even if our problems remain, we do not have to add to those with worries that could make us sick. We can calmly work out a way to solve them without exacerbating them with worry. If we place our worries into God's hands, we can trust in God to help us.

We worry about what people have said or done to us in the past. A solution is to let go of the past and the wrongs done to us by others. By putting our past worries in God's hands, our mind remains clear. This cleanses our mind of toxins associated with past hurts that often lead to anger. When we let God do the worrying, it detoxes our mind and heart to enjoy inner peace.

Why worry about a past we cannot change? A way to help us put past worries into God's hands is to forgive. Whom should we forgive? Those who are parents and children can forgive each other for any hurts by resolving to forget them. Those who are friends or co-workers can forgive each other any misunderstandings by resolving to forget about them from this day forward. It is time to wipe the slate clean and begin anew. This will decrease the number of things we worry about.

What happens if we do not forgive and forget? We worry. Our same dirty laundry is carried into the future. We replay the same old worry movies. We delay our own happiness. Do we want to trade off the bliss within for focusing on worrying about all these people and problems that have brought us down in the past? Wouldn't we rather fill our hearts and souls with joy?

Through meditation, we can stop worrying about a past we cannot change. We can let go of anger. What is the result? We will have clarity of vision to experience happiness within. Do we want to let worrying about another person stand between us and peace? When we dwell on the hurts given to us by another person, we are giving that person the power to stand between us and joy. To detox from misery, we can put our worries into God's hands and forgive and forget. The reward for giving up past worries is we awaken within to spiritual treasures.

We will no longer be thrashing around to stay afloat in life. Instead, we will be floating in the sea of spiritual love. Filled with unending and unspeakable bliss, we will be bathed through every pore of our being with waves after waves of intoxicating love. We will be bubbling over with divine joy. No matter how many problems face us outside, we will be protected and supported from within by bliss. This will carry us through the difficulties of life.

We can do this when we start meditating and stop worrying. The next time we worry, consider whether it is worth the time of our precious lives to engage in thoughts about things that may or may not ever happen. If there is really a danger, then instead of worrying, we should make specific plans to avert the threat. If we take actions, we have done all we can do. We do not need to supplement those actions with worry. Taking action is useful; but worry is useless. We do our best, and then use our remaining time doing something beneficial to others or ourselves. In this way, we can eliminate many of our worries.

From this moment onward, when we open the door of meditation, close off all the outside pains and sorrows. We deposit all the hurts at the outer door. We tell our mind that we need to make a conscious decision to forget all the previous hurts, forgive everyone and everything from the past and let go. In this way, we can spend all our time in enjoyment. The fruits of doing so are that by leaving our worries in God's hands, we are free to be peaceful and happy.

The Gift of Acceptance

We may think that we alone have problems, but troubles afflict everyone. The key is to find a way to deal with them, so they do not bring us down.

In this connection, there is a story from ancient times of a man who was the son of a nobleman, one of the ruling classes in his town. He and his family were wealthy and lived in a palace with all the comforts anyone would want.

One day he met the Buddha and was moved by him and his teachings. During those times, it was different than today where we can pursue a spiritual life without giving up the world and one's family or possessions. In those times, one was expected to renounce one's wealth and position to take up the life of a beggar.

His family was shocked when he told them he was going to give up his life as a nobleman with all his wealth and his heritage to become a disciple and live the life of a beggar. They tried to talk him out of it, but he was determined to find God and believed that was the way to do it.

Saying good-bye to his family, he left his house with just the clothes on his back, his shoes, and a sack with as few belongings as possible to survive life as a beggar.

He had to sleep on the bare ground wherever he could find a spot outdoors. He had to keep a begging bowl for people to offer him food. But he was happy as he was following his wish to devote his life to God.

In the palace, he had lived a pampered life, surrounded by all the comforts of wealth. He was used to sleeping on a soft bed and walking on plush carpeting. He could eat whatever delicacies he wanted and never knew any hunger.

As he proceeded on his journey in search of God, it was not long before sleeping on the hard ground without any comfortable mattress wore on him. His legs and body soon were pained. Having an attack of arthritis, his joints and muscles ached.

In the beginning, he tried to ignore the pain and go on with his spiritual practices. But as days and weeks passed, he could not turn off the pain. He ached so much that it began to disturb his meditative practices.

Soon, he had trouble walking. It was too painful to get around.

The pain was so much that he lost all joy in life. His mind was agitated from the suffering. The peace he had been experiencing when he began his spiritual life started to fade. He was upset all the time and lost his equanimity.

One day, as he was walking through town as he had to find new places to sit and beg for his food, he saw a young girl in the distance playing with her friends. As he got closer to the group, he noticed the girl was hobbling around on crutches.

He said, "That girl looks so happy and is having great fun with her friends. Yet she is on crutches. She looks like she is dancing with joy."

As he got closer, he noticed the girl had only one leg.

"How can she be so happy with only one leg? Still, she is playing and having a good time."

He then became ashamed of himself and said, "This girl with far more suffering than me and who must manage with missing a limb is happier than I am. Here I am, a disciple of the Buddha, who has learned to meditate and go within to realms that are free from sorrow and pain, yet I am complaining about the little pain I have."

He then realized that there are people who suffer far more than he did. Besides that, he had been given a meditative practice to help him gain spiritual consciousness and be in a state beyond the pains and sorrows of life.

This story is a helpful reminder to us whenever we go through life's difficulties. We may think we alone are struggling, but so is everyone else. At times, their problems may even be harder to deal with than ours are.

Those who learn to meditate have a solution to life's hardships. Meditation is a way to help us deal with our problems. Through meditation we focus within so we can ride on a spiritual current that takes us beyond the suffering of life.

Within us is an ocean of all joy and happiness. When we meditate and tap into this sea of bliss, we are temporarily removed from the suffering of the outer world. We go beyond the pains of our physical body. When we merge in the ocean of all love, we find relief from our emotional and mental pains. Meditation can mitigate the pains of our body, mind, and emotions.

Meditation is a practice. In the beginning, we may find it difficult to sit still, to quiet our mind, and stay focused. Many may find that at first, we cannot sit still for long. That becomes easier with practice. Over time we can sit still for a longer period.

Next, we may find we cannot keep our mind still. But with the meditative practice we can still our mind longer. We reach a point where we can still our mind long enough and become proficient enough to be absorbed in the inner Light and Sound. Once we connect with the inner stream of Light and Sound, we can swim in the sea of peace.

Whatever happens in life, by perfecting our meditations to dive into the ocean of bliss, we can deal with our problems in a calm and accepting way.

We should keep going forward, little by little, bit by bit, until we perfect our practice so we can reach that ocean of happiness within. This can remedy life's problems and will give us the gift of acceptance to whatever comes our way.

Then, no matter what happens, we can deal with it better. We learn to live without stress, fear, anxiety, panic, and worry no matter what our lot in life is. Then, nothing can disturb our peace of mind. Contentment stays with us through rain and shine, sickness and health, poverty and wealth, and any other eventuality.

The gift of acceptance coupled with meditation will carry us through life's challenges.

The Medicine of Laughter

In this scientific age, people often lack trust in the wisdom handed down to us from the past by great thinkers, philosophers, and saints. Nowadays, people tend to believe only what is tested in a physical laboratory, confirmed by scientists. Yet, in analyzing recent scientific discoveries we find many prove what was taught in ancient times. In modern times, it is only when something is confirmed by a scientific study that people believe in its veracity. One such study deals with laughter and smiling. Recent medical and mental health professionals report on their importance.

In this connection, there is a true anecdote in the life of an American journalist named Norman Cousins. While traveling overseas in 1964, he developed a fever. His temperature kept rising to dangerous levels. He had to fly home where his pain and fever intensified.

He had to be hospitalized. Soon, he was unable to move his arms or legs. The doctor diagnosed a rare disease called "Collagen," which affected the connective tissue in his body.

The doctors declared that there was little hope for him to survive. Only one in five hundred people lived. They said that it would take only a miracle for him to recover.

Lying there in the hospital, Norman decided he did not just want to give up by giving in to his condition. While his body was unable to move, his brain was still active. He started to analyze the situation.

He said to himself, "If people work under stressful conditions, spend too much time worrying, and suffer anxiety and fear, their health suffers. If that is true, then the opposite must also be true. That means if people are stress-free, cheerful, and filled with hope, optimism, and love, they should overcome any disease."

He decided that if stress, fear, worry, and anxiety pull us down, then happiness, laughter, hope, and love should pull us back up.

Knowing the doctors could not help him, he decided to take matters into his own hands and find a treatment for himself. He thought the cure for him would be laughter.

From that day on, he watched funny movies. He read books about jokes. He found as many ways to make himself laugh as he could. Through watching comedies and reading and telling jokes, his health started to improve.

He continued his regiment of laughter until one day, he no longer needed the medicine the doctors were giving him as their last resort in the hopes those medications would work.

Within a few months, he could move and walk again and was back playing on the golf course. He was able to return to his work as a journalist. To the amazement of his doctors, he was cured.

He ended up writing a book, called *Anatomy of an Illness*, which shocked the medical community. Nobody thought there was therapeutic value in laughter.

Today, the role laughter and smiling have on our health is now accepted. Medical researchers have explored the muscles in the face that relate to smiling. They discovered it takes more work to use the muscles to frown and look angry than it does to smile.

Studies on the value of laughter reveal that laughing releases hormones such as endorphins that have the power to make us feel happy. When flooded with these chemicals produced by our own body, they raise our spirits and fortify our immune system. Thus, when we smile, our immune system is stronger, and we are better able to resist disease.

Similarly, if we are already ill, but we stay positive and happy, some medical researchers report that we can cut down the time of our illness and heal faster. That is one reason doctors are promoting meditation, especially to speed up healing. Studies have been done to show that relaxation and meditation can speed up recovery. Why? They put us in a state of calm in which the body produces hormones that make us feel good. This aids the healing process.

Humor is a wonderful way to dispel a tense situation. It is a way of changing anger into laughter. It helps relieve the pressure of life and puts us in a relaxed state.

In this connection, there was a true incident from the life of President Abraham Lincoln. Being wise, people would come to him to settle an argument. He had a knack for settling disputes.

Two men were having a heated argument for hours. They were fighting over the correct proportion that the length of a man's legs should be to the size of his body. They decided to go to Lincoln to settle the question.

After listening to both sides of the argument, Lincoln listened to both sides with thoughtfulness. He then asked them, as if in a court room, to summarize their cases.

After hearing their summaries, he said with dry humor, "This argument must have been highly debated many times in the past. I am sure that it was so hotly debated that there must have been blood shed over who was right and who was wrong. You are arguing such an important topic that I am undergoing great mental anguish in trying to reach a decision as a final judgment on this case."

After a few moments, he said with great wit, "My opinion is that when we sweep away all sides of the issue, the answer is that a man's legs should be at least long enough to reach from his body to the ground."

The two men could not help but break out in laughter to end their dispute.

This historical anecdote shows how laughter can be used to settle a tense situation. The men were arguing so strongly as if the issue were life and death. Lincoln, as a calm third-party observer, could see what a ridiculous topic they were arguing. To lighten the situation, he used humor.

Humor is a healer. It helps us deal with the worries that the strains of life bring. When problems mount, we become so wrapped up in them that we may become sad or depressed. These emotions are the mind's way of keeping us tied to the world. When we laugh, though, we detach ourselves from sorrows. We can separate ourselves from the tense situation, even if briefly, and connect with the joy within.

Laughing has a component to our mental health. Those same happy hormones can keep us feeling mentally good. This can help turn around the feeling of being in the doldrums. Life hands each of us problems. No one is immune from difficulties. We may think we alone are filled with worries but listen to the tale of every person and each suffers as much as we do in our own way. It is said that if everyone put their problems into a pile in the middle of the earth and were asked to pick a set of problems from that pile, after examining the problems of others, each would pick his or her own problem again. We would realize that others' circumstances are not much better than our own, and sometimes they may even be worse.

Once we realize that problems are a part of life, we can either choose to be depressed and go about with a shadow of sadness surrounding us, or we can be content. Our problem may not go away immediately, but we can face them boldly. When we have a difficulty, sadness creates a secondary problem because our mental state is agitated and our immune system weakens. If we remain jolly, we only have one problem to deal with without the addition of sadness.

Laughter helps us connect to the inner state of spiritual love. When in a state of love, we are happy. Love and joy are our true nature. When we identify with that true essence, we are blissful.

Through meditation we can live each day with laughter and smiles. As we tap into our inner essence we can spread joy to others, who in turn also radiate happiness. This cycle of smiling and laughter can detox the world and make it a more joyous place for all

The Necessity of Detoxing our Mind from Toxins

The list of toxins is long. Life is filled with challenges that trigger the release of these barriers to our equanimity. Is there any hope to lead life free of these poisons that sap our state of peace?

Meditation provides solutions to deal with these toxins. If we learn simple meditation on the inner Light and Sound to detox our mind, we can pass through life's difficulties in a state of calm, peace, and joy.

Exercise: Review any notes you made from the exercises in these chapters in which you reflected on toxins you ever suffered from mentally. Then make a list of which ones you want to detox from your mind. If there are more than one, make a priority list. You

may want to tackle one at a time and work through the solutions described in this book. Then, take another toxin and work through those relevant portions of the book to conquer that one. Alternatively, you can work on several at a time to detox yourself as you read those chapters of the book. Once you learn the process of detoxing your mind, it can become a part of you that you can use repeatedly in your life in your quest for peace and happiness.

PART 4:

A New You:

How to Live a Peaceful, Happy Life

CHAPTER 18:

A New You: Enjoy Life Free of Mental Toxins

Secrets of Cleaning

It is difficult to go through life without some accident or spill that lands on our clothing, our carpet, our furniture, or our cars. We try hard to eat without getting food on us. The harder we try, it inevitably happens that soup or sauce lands on us, staining our new clothes. We try to make it across the carpet with hot tea or coffee, and boom—we trip, and the liquid flies out of our hand, staining the rug. We get a new car and try hard to park it far enough away from the car in the next parking spot, only to find that despite our best efforts, someone swung open his or her car door too widely and it nicked our shiny new car.

Finding ways to keep our belongings clean is a big business for companies and consultants. They invent products and techniques to clean out stains to make everything we own look as good as new. Commercials on home shopping networks display every possible gizmo and gadget to clean our belongings. Books and articles from cleaning experts offer tips on cleaning and removing stains. People devise hundreds of new techniques and products for cleaning our homes, cars, offices, and our bodies.

What about cleaning our mind and our soul? If we could devote the time we spend to cleaning our physical bodies and the world around us to cleaning our mind and soul, we would find invaluable benefits.

In this connection, there is a story of a man who lived alone. As he aged, his eyesight grew weaker. He had always loved admiring his garden. The mature trees with the fullness of their limbs and branches laden with large green leaves brought him joy. Bushes with their seasonal flowers delighted him. Many varieties of flowers bloomed at different times of year, so there was always a kaleidoscope of colors to attract him. He took joy in watching colorful birds flit from tree to tree and seeing squirrels and rabbits scurry across the lawn.

However, he became gloomy when he could no longer see the beauties of nature when he looked out his window. He grew depressed that his failing eyesight prevented him from enjoying the garden and world outside his window.

One day he went to a meeting of senior citizens in his area. They shared stories of their struggles with their aging and failing health. When his turn came, he expressed disappointment in his diminishing eyesight that stopped him from enjoying the beauty through his windows.

One perceptive woman listened with compassion and said, "I have an idea on how to help you." She arranged to come to his house to see what the problem was.

On the day of the appointed visit, she showed up with a big cleaning bucket, mop, broom, cloths, and cleaning detergents. She had wrapped a scarf around her head and was in cleaning clothes.

The man said, "I don't recognize you. Who are you?"

She said, "I am the woman from the senior group who told you I would meet you to see what the problem was that you are having with your vision." He then realized it was her but dressed in cleaning clothes.

She entered and looked around the house.

"Show me the windows you enjoy looking out from to see your garden," she said. He took her to the living room window, where he had his special chair facing the lawn. The woman took her finger and swiped the glass with it.

She then held out her finger. "Look at this," she said. "Your window is filled with dust and grime." She wiped off her finger and then proceeded to take her supplies to clean the windows. She scrubbed the windows and wiped them dry with a cloth.

When she was done, the windows were spotless and clear.

She told him to sit down in his special chair and look out the window.

"How did you do this? I can see my beautiful garden again," he exclaimed with joy.

She then beautifully told him, "It was not your eyesight that was growing dim. The problem was that you allowed your windows to get dirty."

This story describes what happens to each of us. For those in search of seeing God in this lifetime, we need to have clear vision. It is not that God is not there for us, or that we are failing in our abilities to find God. The problem is that we have allowed our inner windows to become dirty.

There is a clear opening we all have at the seat of the soul between and behind the two eyebrows. That is an opening that we have from the moment we are born into this world until our time is up. Through that opening we can have unclouded vision of the wonders within. The problem is that the opening is covered with dust and grime. For that reason, people believe they are unable to experience the spiritual treasures within.

Meditation can clear that opening so we can experience our spiritual wealth. Meditation is the cleaning cloth to eliminate the grime that blocks our vision. Meditation is a process of detoxing our mind. The mind fills that opening with thoughts that distract us. We are always thinking of the past or future. We are thinking of past regrets and future worries. We are caught up in thoughts of anger, hatred, selfishness, and ego. These cause the dust and grime to obstruct our inner vision. Meditation is the process of stilling our mind from these thoughts so we can see the inner vistas.

Along with that, we can do introspection. This is where we practice what the woman in the story did when she visited the house of the man. She came to inspect and assess the situation to find out why he could not see the garden outside. It was not

due to the failing eyesight but due to him allowing dust to accumulate on the window.

Similarly, through introspection, we can assess what is clut-
tering our inner vision. Are we obstructing our vision due to angry
thoughts, words, and deeds? Are we egotistical and criticizing
others for being less wealthy, less powerful, less intelligent, or
less beautiful than we are? Are we separating ourselves from
others due to prejudice, hatred, and bigotry? Are we refusing to
help others in need?

If we find the cause of the grime blocking our vision within,
we can then take steps to remediate the problem. We can pull
out our cleaning supplies and get to work to clear our vision. We
can take steps each day to reduce the grime we accumulate
daily. Each day we can improve by one less speck of grime than
we added the day before. We can note down our goals and our
numbers of failings each day.

How can we reduce the number of spots on our glass from
day to day?

The helping factors for doing so are meditation, introspection, and selfless service. In meditation, we still our mind of
thoughts. This automatically reduces the grime we can accumulate. Contact with the inner Light and Sound is like a cleaning
fluid. It fills us with love and kindness. Thus, when we connect
with the Light and Sound it has the effect of cleaning the window
of our mind.

Doing introspection alerts us to what is causing grime so we
can make an action plan to lessen those spots each day. Reading,
listening to, or watching inspirational messages motivate us to
take action to keep our inner windows clean. Selfless service is a

DETOX THE MIND

chance to clean our window. While doing service without wanting material reward for ourselves, we are not engaged in thinking, speaking, or doing anything that adds grime to our vision. We are working with a still mind, loving heart, and hands open to help others. If done accurately, we are preventing ourselves from adding dust to our windows.

These actions can clear our windows. We can develop our own personal plan to keep our windows clean. We can do so by meditating more and spending time doing selfless service. Studying inspirational works can motivate us to detox our mind. By doing all these things, we will find that like the woman in the story who cleaned the man's windows, we too will clean our own inner windows to enjoy spiritual love.

Choose Our Own Condition

It is a common tendency to blame others for our unhappiness. The offices of psychologists, therapists, and social workers are filled with people who visit for help in solving relationship problems. A good portion of the therapy sessions is spent on the patients or clients complaining about how those around them are making their lives miserable. People complain about how their spouses or partners are causing their unhappiness. Parents complain about their children. Children complain about their parents. People have difficulties even with their close friends. Then, there are difficulties we have at work with our superiors, co-workers, and subordinates. We feel our sorrows are caused by everyone else.

In this connection, there is story about a monk trying to find God. He felt he gained as much as he could on his own but

204

wanted to go further. He went to a saint for help in attaining enlightenment. This happened during past times in the East, when it was common for those studying under a spiritual teacher to live at an ashram. While nowadays many people go to an ashram for short periods of time, in the past it was common to leave one's home to live continually at an ashram.

This monk had to live in close proximity with other students. They would eat meals together, meditate, and do selfless service. Unfortunately, this monk had a bad temper. It did not take much for others to set him off into a tantrum. Sometimes, he would get so mad, he would fly into a rage. His anger was destroying the peaceful atmosphere.

One day, the monk told the fellow students, "What is wrong with this place? The vibrations here are so terrible. Why aren't you all calm, since you are studying under a spiritual teacher? I came here to find peace and grow spiritually, but instead this place is radiating only anger."

The other disciples listened and were shocked at what he was saying. When he had gone outside, they gathered together and said, "This man is always angry at us. Yet he is saying that we are causing the negative atmosphere. He is the one upsetting everyone else."

They tried even harder to help the monk be calm and happy. Yet, anytime he was upset by anything, he would become enraged. The others tried hard not to react, to make sure they were not ruining the peace of the ashram. Yet no matter how hard they tried to remain calm, the monk blamed them as the cause for his anger.

One day, the monk was so upset with them he said, "I don't

find any peace here. You are all terrible disciples as you are causing all kinds of negativity here. I am going to leave here and find
enlightenment by meditating alone in the forest."

The monk packed his belongings and set out to find a quiet
spot in nature to pursue his spiritual growth on his own.

For the first few weeks, he felt peaceful. He enjoyed the soli-
tude of the forest. Nature provided him a calming atmosphere.
He felt he had made a good decision to leave the ashram and
all those people who were upsetting him. Now, he could meditate and live in peace so as to make spiritual progress. The man
was filled with happiness.

One day, he went to the river to collect drinking water in a
clay pot. When he got to the river, he set down the clay pot on
a rock. As he leaned down to scoop water from the river, the
pot toppled over. He let the water in his hands spill out to stand
the pot back up. He again reached down to dip his hands in the
water to scoop it out, and while doing so, the pot fell over again.
He had to let go of the water and reset the pot. This went on a
few more times, until he became furious.

"What kind of useless pot are you? You keep falling over,"
he shouted. He lifted the pot and smashed it on the rock,
shattering it.

Now, the only vessel he had to collect water was ruined. He
had no other pot to use. With no one to shout at, he sat down
and became downhearted.

He thought to himself, "I left the ashram because everyone
there was making me angry. There is no one here in the forest
but me, and yet I am still angry. The anger I thought I was leaving
behind at the ashram has accompanied me here. It is not the

people who are the cause of my anger. It must be the anger in me that has caused all the problems."

The monk realized that all this time he was blaming everyone else for his bad temper. Now, with no one to blame, and the anger still a part of his life, he awakened to the truth. Anger is not caused by people and situations around us. It is our own reactions to the people and situations in our life that result in our anger.

The lesson the monk learned can also help us. If we replace the time we spend complaining about people and situations that upset us, and instead use it to analyze our reactions to them, we can overcome our anger. People are going to do what they do. We cannot control others. However, we can learn to control our own reactions to their behaviors.

Take the example of weather. We expect it to be sunny, but it rains. We think it is summer, but we have chilly days or hail. We think it is going to be cold out, and suddenly the weather turns hot. We can either be upset about the weather changes, or we can bring with us a variety of adaptive clothing, so we are prepared for the heat and cold, the rain and the sun. We still have to live our lives, no matter what the weather is. We still have to eat our meals, go to work, take care of our families, and do all other activities each day. We may notice the weather, but we try not to let it stop us from our plans.

In the same way, people around us have their good days and bad days. Sometimes people are pleasant to us, and sometimes due to their own problems they act moody or upset. That should not determine what our day is like. If we let other people influence whether we are happy or sad, there is no end to our problems. Why should we let someone else's mood or behavior dictate whether we have a joyful day or a miserable one?

The monk realized that it was not the other people causing him to be angry. It was his own reaction to them that caused his temper. Enlightenment finally dawned on him when he realized that even when he was alone, he was a victim of his own anger. He had no one to blame. Realizing the anger was coming from his own self, he was able to change for the better and control his temper.

People who go to counselors to complain that the cause of their problems is their partner, often find that when they leave one partner, the same problems follow them to their next relationship. Sometimes, after being with three or four different partners, we discover the other person behaves just as poorly as the first one we left. Over time, we come to see that it is not the other person causing the problem: it is us, who keep reacting to others in the same way, making our own selves angry. Then, when we look back, we realize that each partner was a different person, but it is we who are the ones who could not control our anger no matter who we were with.

The same may happen when we have a boss who we find difficult. We leave a job because we do not like the boss, but find we are angry no matter which new boss we get. We realize over time that it is not the boss who is getting us angry. It is the anger within ourselves that we cannot control that reacts to each person for whom we work. The boss and situation are different, but we are in the habit of responding with the same lack of control over our own reactions.

When working with others, we have a golden opportunity to use it as a training ground to conquer our anger. Anger is one of the hindrances to our spiritual growth. Daily we introspect on how many times we get angry, with the aim to reduce that number day by day. Ultimately, we should reach a point where we have zero failures in anger. When we are engaged with others, there will be many times things won't go our way. Someone will say or do something we do not like or agree with. Each time that happens, we have an opportunity to remember the story of the monk. We can choose our own condition. Do we want to let others upset us and ruin our own day? Or do we want to observe what they do but not let it affect us to the point where we become angry? We have a choice. We are not helpless victims of others' moods. We can choose to remain calm, cool, and collected.

Being calm does not mean we ignore the problems others cause. We still need to be active and take steps to resolve problems. We can even offer a calming presence to help them cool down. Spirituality is not a passive road, but an active one. We still must live in the world and help make things better. But adding anger to the mix does not help anyone. We can calmly deal with other people and situations without succumbing to anger. We can take steps to make situations better and help those around us deal with the difficulties that are upsetting them. Yet we can do so in a way that allows us to keep control over our own selves.

Just as when cold winds blow on what was supposed to be a sunny day, instead of being upset, we calmly put on a jacket; so we can deal with the winds of other people's anger by calmly putting on the protective coat of nonviolence.

When dressed for chilly weather and a sudden rise in temperature makes us hot, we remove our outer layers. Similarly, when our environment is cool and collected, but someone else's anger raises the heat in the room, we can calmly remove our own layer of anger to stay peaceful.

It is the same with all the toxins. How can we learn to detox our mind from all poisons and choose peace instead? The secret to gaining control over ourselves is meditation. By sitting in meditation, we are tapping into a peaceful place within ourselves. If we find we are in a situation where toxins erupt, we can stop them. If we can temporarily remove ourselves to go to another room or space, meditate until we are calm, and then return, we can train ourselves to control our mental poisons. This will help put our attention on the place of peace within to divert us from the negative situation.

Over time, when we meditate more and more, we naturally will be kept calm from within even in the face of situations that threaten to upset us. We can then calmly find a strategy to help the situation become better. When in the throes of toxic stimuli, we can focus on solving problems instead of being caught up in reacting to them. Through meditation, we can gain the stability to deal with life in the best possible manner. We can then be conscious enough to choose our own condition. Do we want to be miserable, or do we want to be peaceful and happy? We have the choice to decide. Meditation can help us choose peace and happiness by detoxing our mind.

Exercise: Review this book and note down which toxins affect your own peace and happiness. Study the methods suggested in each chapter showing how to detox your mind from those poisons. Then make an action plan to remove those toxins. Take each toxin, one at a time, and work at removing its effects. When one is removed, begin work on another. Note how your mind grows more peaceful with time. Keep working at it until one day you wake up to a life free from stress, fear, anxiety, worry, and depression. You can arise each day filled with peace and joy.

About the Author

Sant Rajinder Singh is an author and internationally recognized spiritual Master of meditation on the inner Light and Sound. He is head of Science of Spirituality, with over 3,200 centers in fifty countries that provides a forum for people to learn meditation. He is a best-selling author whose many books, translated into fifty-six languages, include *Meditation as Medication for the Soul, Inner and Outer Peace through Meditation,* and *Building Bridges through Meditation.* He also has many CDs, DVDs, and hundreds of articles published in magazines, newspapers, and journals and has appeared on TV, radio, and Internet broadcasts worldwide, and on social media.

He received a B.Tech Degree in Electrical Engineering from I.I.T. (Indian Institute of Technology), Madras, India, in 1967; received an M.S. Degree in Electrical Engineering from I.I.T (Illinois Institute of Technology), Chicago, Illinois, in 1970; and was awarded a Special I.I.T. Fellowship. He had a successful twenty-year career in engineering, communications, and technology, including one of the world's leading communication companies. For his accomplishments in the fields of peace and spirituality, he received a Distinguished Leadership Award from Illinois Institute of Technology, Chicago, Illinois.

His work in the fields of science, computers, and communication has given him the ability to have a scientific approach to spirituality. He makes the science of spirituality and the practice of meditation easy for people to understand and practice for themselves. He holds meditation seminars, gives public lectures, and hosts international conferences, presenting his powerful, yet simple meditation on the inner

Light and Sound to millions throughout the world. He has also presented the benefits of meditation to medical practitioners including the National Institutes of Health, All India Institute of Medical Sciences, and universities such as Harvard University; the University of California, Berkeley; I.I.T Madras (Chennai); I.I.T. Delhi; I.I.T. Mumbai; and chapters of Hospice. Many doctors have learned the meditation technique from him and use this regularly with their patients. Civic and social leaders have recognized his spiritual and humanitarian work with numerous awards and tributes. His life has been one continuous thread of service to humanity to bring about a world of peace, unity, and spiritual upliftment.

For more information about
Sant Rajinder Singh, contact:

Radiance Publishers
1042 Maple Ave., Lisle, IL 60532
sales@radiancepublishers.com
www.radiancepublishers.com